KATIE BROWN
decorates

5 STYLES 10 ROOMS 105 PROJECTS

KATIE BROWN
decorates

5 STYLES 10 ROOMS 105 PROJECTS

KATIE BROWN

photographs by PAUL WHICHELOE

design by DINA DELL'ARCIPRETE HOUSER

HarperResource

An Imprint of HarperCollinsPublishers

Other Books by Katie Brown

Katie Brown Entertains

KATIE BROWN decorates

For information, address HarperCollins Publishers Inc.,
10 East 53rd Street, New York, NY 10022.
HarperCollins books may be purchased for educational, business,
or sales promotional use. For information please write:
Special Markets Department, HarperCollins Publishers Inc.,
10 East 53rd Street, New York, NY 10022.

FIRST EDITION

Designed by Dina Dell'Arciprete Houser

Library of Congress Cataloging-in-Publication Data
Brown, Katie.
    Katie Brown decorates : 5 styles 10 rooms 105 projects / Katie Brown ;
photographs by Paul Whicheloe ; design by Dina Dell'Arciprete Houser
        p. cm.
    ISBN 0-06-271616-6
    1. handcraft. 2. Interior decoration—Amateurs' manuals. I. Title.
TT157 .B78497 2002
747—dc21

02 03 04 05 06 WBC/TP 10 9 8 7 6 5 4 3 2 1

This book is dedicated to two of my heroes.

The Miller family for the selfless, graceful act of taking a young girl
named Linda into their home and giving her peace.

To that girl named Linda who in turn created a home for me that never
stopped being colorful, constant, and forever nurturing.

CONTENTS

ACKNOWLEDGMENTS

I cannot even begin to understand why the people who created this book hung in there, but they did and I am forever grateful.

Dina, thank you for all the tears, long train rides, and power tools.

Erinn, who knew the horse behind would take the lead so quickly.

Luis, your undying spirit inspires me daily.

Heather, your hot food kept us going.

Victoria, your concern and organization made me able to work harder.

Kerri, I think you know the amount of support I continually feel from my hometown girl.

Eric, if you could just give me one ounce of your grace and class I would smile wider.

Paul, your calm made it all possible.

Dina, the designer, for simply being soooo good.

Lon, Sean, Ari, and the rest of Endeavor, you have guided me and my sometimes less than ladylike moods with a steady hand.

Patti and Fred, will you continue to call me "boss"?

The unbelievable helpful staff at Lowe's in Middletown, New York, who just kept loading up our U-Hauls with as much enthusiasm for our project as we felt.

Jo-Ann etc. in West Nyack, New York, you have an unmatchable selection of all the things necessary to finish off the projects in this book.

Peter Corbuzzi and the team at Lenox for their continual support.

Ikea, in Elizabeth, New Jersey, the store that gave us accessible-yet-high-design elements that complemented our goals.

Sanderson Fabrics in New York City, finding your fabrics and using them to produce these projects adds greatly to the look of each room.

And Christy, your patience and evenness will continually allow me to go higher.

Mostly, to my friends and family for understanding my sporadic disappearances that were necessary to fulfill my goals.

Thank you.

Our favorite Luis Rivera

Creative consultants (left to right)
Erinn Heilman, Dina Manfre,
Kerri Mertaugh, and Alex Levine

I wrote this book because I love daydreaming about the space around me. Colors, textures, objects, and light all influence who I am, how I feel, how I work, and how I live. Often when I wake up in the morning, before I open my eyes, I imagine that I'm in Paris, or in a big farmhouse, or maybe even on top of a snowy mountain in a log cabin. Then I realize that I am in the same place I was the night before: in my room, in my house, on my street, in my town. Not a bad place to be if you have invested in where you live. But how? How does this happen when you have little time and money?

For answers, I turn to books, magazines, and museums, spending much of my time poring through these sources of inspiration. I sit; I stare; I think, how can I create that? There is one problem, though: Many of these photographs or exhibits don't start with an idea; they start with great architecture—an eighteenth-century castle is restored, a downtown loft is gutted and made chic, a lake house with views for miles and a horse barn to match are featured in a magazine. How's a girl to find hope? With four simple walls, can I achieve the stark sleek style of a downtown loft, the homeyness of a seaside cabin, the playfulness of a children's clubhouse? I say yes! You just need an idea—an idea of the look you want—and then you need to find the projects that fit.

This book attempts to prove my point. In each of the five sections, we transform two basic rooms—a bedroom and a living room—using different decorating themes

INTRODUCTION

and filling the rooms with similarly styled elements. To begin, we brainstormed for the essentials of any room, such as curtains, slipcovers, wall and floor treatments, lighting, and smaller decorating touches. Then we selected the different looks, ranging from city chic to cabin. Slowly the rooms began to evolve. They became rooms with a point of view. They became five styles with distinctive looks, achieved by making several do-it-yourself design pieces.

So, again, the answer to the question is yes. You can start with four simple walls and an idea and wake up in exactly the right place, right where you live. Use this book for inspiration. Use this book as a resource book—a book chock-full of ideas to help you build your own special environment. We designed the individual projects to fit the styles we chose, but don't limit yourself. Think Geranimals: mix and match. For example, create a floor covering from one room and combine it with a wall treatment from another room. We've also included a project list at the front of the book, so if you have a particular piece of furniture or a wall or a floor that needs help, this list will give you a sneak peek at the treatments we offer you. Remember that you can adjust the color, texture, or fabric to whatever suits you. There are no rules, no combinations that are "right," just suggestions and ideas that can be adjusted for your own dreams. Do not let four simple walls, little money, and little time discourage you from creating the look that makes you want to be just right where you are.

Furniture

→ To make rooms more flexible, include some movable pieces such as ottomans, stools, and occasional chairs.

→ To draw attention to your favorite piece of furniture, don't overaccessorize or crowd it with other pieces.

→ To make a room more inviting, avoid shoving furniture against walls.

→ To make a room cozy, when you are arranging furniture, think of it in groups rather than as individual pieces, floating.

→ To create a focal point, use one large piece of furniture rather than several small pieces.

→ To keep a room fresh, rearrange the furniture several times a year.

Floors

→ To make a room seem bigger, keep the floor covering or treatment the same throughout.

→ To create separate areas in an open space, use matching area rugs to suggest room dividers while keeping consistency.

→ When redecorating a room, start with the floors.

→ To unclutter a room, leave the floors alone except for a good polish.

Walls

→ To add personality to a room, wall color is the easiest and least expensive option.

→ To make a room more intimate, paint the walls a darker color.

→ To make a room seem spacious, paint the walls a light color.

→ To tone down a sun-filled room, paint the walls a pale color.

→ To reassure yourself about using bright colors, remember that there are no bad ones.

→ To complete a room after you have painted the walls, look up and choose a color for the ceiling.

→ To decide whether or not you like a new wall color, live with it for at least two days and get used to it.

→ To make walls seem bigger, paint the crown and base molding in a shade similar or identical to the color of your walls.

→ To make a room feel larger, hang mirrors on the walls.

→ To finish off the walls, remember to hang pictures in clusters rather than dotted throughout the room.

SOME THOUGHTS TO KEEP IN MIND
when putting a room together

Windows

→ To make a ceiling seem higher, hang curtains far above the window and as close to the ceiling as possible.
→ To choose the length of curtains, remember that sill-length curtains are more informal than those that puddle on the floor. Length adds drama.
→ To determine the desired width of curtains, measure the width of the window and then multiply the number by three.
→ To highlight an architecturally ornate window, keep it unobstructed by using simple window covering.
→ To help create a calm and unified room, use matching window treatments.

Lighting

→ To make a room look less staged, always burn your new candles a little before you put them into candleholders.
→ To encourage light to travel throughout a room, use reflective surfaces.
→ To change the mood of a room, install dimmer switches.
→ To foster a welcoming feeling in a room, have more than just overhead lighting.
→ To create a warm environment, use lightbulbs of different intensity.
→ To produce a room that looks comfortably lived in, place fixtures at different heights throughout the space. For example, use a floor lamp as well as overhead and table lights.
→ To design your lighting look, think of light in three different ways:
  background lighting / task lighting / overhead lighting
→ To add light to a room, add mirrors.

Accessories

→ To add the finishing touches to a room, imagine that you are adding layers, or accessorizing, just as you would an outfit with jewelry, scarves, and so on.
→ To create aesthetic arrangements, place an odd number of objects together.
→ To determine the placement of objects, try placing items with similar themes together.
→ To hang photographs, keep in mind that grouping all black-and-white photos together and all color photos together looks best.
→ To avoid overaccessorizing, eliminate a lot of the small pieces.
→ To keep a room interesting, occasionally switch or rearrange your pieces. Think of them as similar to museum collections, which are always revolving.

PROJECT LIST

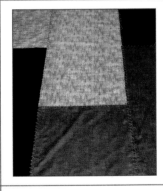

169
Deep Blue Sea
Enchanted August

215
Home Turf
Through the Looking Glass

191
Tiptoe Through the Tulips
Enchanted August

239
Sole Mate
Through the Looking Glass

WALLS

PROJECT LIST

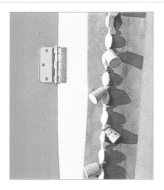

WALLS

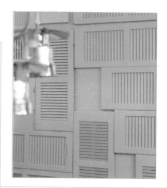

131
Home Sweet Home
Cabin Fever

192
Shutterbug
Enchanted August

150
Tree House
Cabin Fever

215
The Hole Story
Through the Looking Glass

154
Bandana-Rama
Cabin Fever

241
Stripe Up the Band (top)
Through the Looking Glass

170
Gathering Shells
Enchanted August

241
Stripe Up the Band (bottom)
Through the Looking Glass

PROJECT LIST

174
Dreamcatcher
Enchanted August

174
Dreamcatcher
Enchanted August

216
Rigged for Romping
Through the Looking Glass

225
Flying Trapeze
Through the Looking Glass

200
Rows of Hose
Enchanted August

PROJECT LIST

42
Bed Bundle
Street Chic

45
Silk Roll
Street Chic

67
Unattached
Street Chic

91
Tie One On
Pick a Color

92
Pillow with a Waistline
Pick a Color

109
Check Your Pockets
Pick a Color

110
Rough Rider
Pick a Color

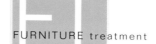

135
Mad About Plaid
Cabin Fever

135
Tucked Inn
Cabin Fever

137
Buckle Up
Cabin Fever

155
Cover Up
Cabin Fever

158
Rocky Top
Cabin Fever

PROJECT LIST

PROJECT LIST

FURNITURE treatment

221
Rickracktoe
Through the Looking Glass

242
Clearly Covered
Through the Looking Glass

222
Happy Bed Skirt!
Through the Looking Glass

245
On Contact!
Through the Looking Glass

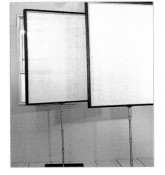
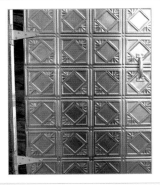

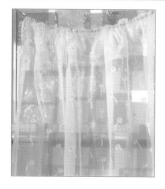

PROJECT LIST

51
Hanging Hats
Street Chic

118
Shades of Light
Pick a Color

71
Industrial Strength
Street Chic

142
Hot Socks
Cabin Fever

72
Wok This Way
Street Chic

184
Knotical
Enchanted August

96
Pitching Pictures
Pick a Color

205
Rake It In
Enchanted August

L	A

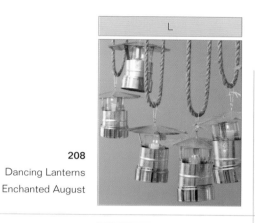

208

Dancing Lanterns

Enchanted August

54

Suspended

Street Chic

232

Wet Paint! Bright Lights!

Through the Looking Glass

54

Steel Frame

Street Chic

233

Button Up

Through the Looking Glass

76

Pillow Perfect

Street Chic

249

Battery-Operated

Through the Looking Glass

76

Nature's Bounty

Street Chic

PROJECT LIST

PROJECT LIST

STREET CHIC
a downtown loft

It was one of those one-of-a-kind, "I can't believe it happened to me" stories, like a winning number in lotto, or love at first sight, or Charlie's golden ticket. My story was finding a huge New York loft—rent-free! I was a twenty-two-year-old actress, waitressing, with barely enough cash to pay a cable bill, yet I had procured a loft the size of a gymnasium with an outdoor space to boot.

Let me back up and explain: In my lean postcollege years, I had been living on Manhattan's Upper East Side. I had been friendly with my landlord, Joe, who had a workshop in the basement. (I would often watch him sand, buff, polish, and bring back to life gorgeous antiques, his hands always swollen from the hard work and discolored by the dark furniture stain.) One day, I told Joe that it was time for me to move away from the Upper East Side—as an "artist," I felt I needed to be downtown. Joe smiled and told me to call his friend Ivan, who was from his hometown in Yugoslavia. Ivan had just bought a loft building in the East Village, and maybe he could help. The building he bought did have an empty floor, but it needed, uh, some work: The only running water was in a sink that leaked, in the center of a big empty space. I could stay for a time, because he was trying to convert the building, but he would not put up any money for improvements.

No kitchen? No problem. I thought I could renovate the apartment myself (why, I don't know, because I had never renovated anything before). However, building a home from scratch became exhilarating: I got to know all about Sheetrock. I bought my first tool belt, and electric drills no longer scared me. I befriended a man on the street who would let me know when an abandoned bathtub

was found on the Bowery. Next came sinks, countertops, tables, and cabinets—all from the street! I also enlisted the help of my friends. Greg, the "acting" carpenter, was my savior, and there were several others. I truly built a house with the help of friends, the street, and a new attention to anything scrappy.

From a packing-paper wall covering to a Chinese wok lamp, the stuff that makes up New York City taught me well. Ivan, Greg, Joe, the man who told me about the tub, and the city that sheltered them all contributed to my development as an urban homemaker. I also gained a fondness for all things city and all things tough. My loft may not have been genteel, but it was a reflection of the time when I was a young waitress-actress and Joe was my winning lotto ticket, Greg was my love, and Ivan was my Willy Wonka.

This chapter pays homage to my first days in New York City and my first days of taking someone else's junk and turning it into *my* treasure. May it help you do the same.

BEDROOM

Grass Underfoot **floors**

The Great Wall **walls**

Steeling Wainscoting **walls**

Mondrian Metal **furniture structure**

Elevated **furniture structure**

Bed Bundle **furniture treatment**

Silk Roll **furniture treatment**

Washboard Shelves **furniture structure**

A Meshy Situation **windows**

Hanging Hats **lighting**

Suspended **accessories**

Steel Frame **accessories**

Grass Underfoot

I've found all sorts of great things to use as floor and wall coverings, but one of my favorite materials to work with is sisal. It has great texture and really keeps the minimalist look of a room. Sisal can be pretty expensive, though, so for this project we found a great alternative—grass mat. It also has a great texture, and the best part is that it's inexpensive and easy to find.

Supplies

Grass mats
¼-inch foam rubber (as much as you need to cover the back of the grass mats)
Muslin

Tools

Hot glue gun and glue sticks
Spray adhesive
Scissors
Tape measure

Getting Started

1. To determine how many mats you will need, measure the area you want to cover. (Our mats were 3 × 5 inches.)
2. Cut the foam rubber to match the length and width of the grass mats, minus 1 inch on all four sides to give it a more finished look.
3. Place two mats upside down and side by side on the floor.
4. Cut the muslin strip to the length of the grass mats, making sure it's wide enough to act as a piece of tape that will hold the two mats together. (The strip should be approximately 3 inches wide.)
5. Using the glue gun, attach a muslin strip to where the two mats meet, sealing the two mats together. Let dry.
6. Using spray adhesive, spray the back of the mats evenly.
7. Attach the foam rubber to the mats. Let dry.
8. Repeat this process with as many mats as needed to create a square or rectangular area rug that reaches almost to the perimeter of the room.
9. Put them into place.

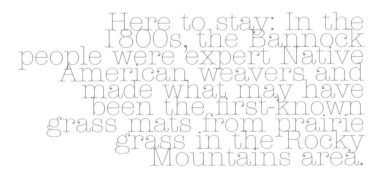

Here to stay: In the 1800s, the Bannock people were expert Native American weavers and made what may have been the first-known grass mats from prairie grass in the Rocky Mountains area.

The Great Wall

One of the great things about living in downtown New York in the early 1990s was watching old warehouses being turned into lofts. High ceilings, large windows, and tons of aluminum and steel, the new Sheetrock for that time. The walls in this project are reminiscent of those funky downtown lofts.

Supplies
Corrugated aluminum sheet metal
3-inch sheet metal screws

Tools
Screw gun
Tape measure

Keep it simple: Pick one wall that you want to highlight with your metal panels, because sheet metal can look overpowering when used on every wall.

Getting Started
1. Measure the wall you want to cover. (It will be easiest to cover a wall that does not have any molding or windows to work around.)
2. Using the wall's measurements, buy enough panels of corrugated aluminum sheet to cover the area.
3. Starting at the top corner of the wall and working your way down to the floor, attach each piece, using a screw gun and screws (one screw in each corner should suffice).

Steeling Wainscoting

Let's continue our love affair with sheet metal and, while we're at it, update the look of wainscoting.

Supplies
Aluminum sheet metal
Metal doorjambs

Tools
Hammer
Nails
Tape measure

Getting Started
1. Measure 36 inches up from the floor, and the length of the wall you want to cover.
2. Using these measurements, roll out and cut the sheet metal.
3. Nail panels to the wall.
4. Along the top of your panels, nail strips of metal doorjambs across the entire length of the wall, for a decorative look.

Mondrian Metal

The head (f the board of directors, the captain of the team, the squad leader, a headboard . . . what do these all have in common? Each is the boss, each has the last say, each makes the first impression, each is the tone setter. Okay, you might think it's a stretch to compare a boss to a headboard, but I swear that a headboard, and a headboard alone, can determine the feel of the room. So if you do nothing else to your room, experiment with the look of the headboard.

Supplies

Aluminum sheet metal
½-inch-thick plywood
Galvanized patching squares
Metal screens for covering ducts
Metal upholstery tacks
Aluminum corner edging
Liquid nails
4 heavy-duty screw hooks

Tools

Screw gun and screws
Staple gun and staples
Hammer
Matte knife
Tape measure

Getting Started

1. Measure the width of the bed.
2. Using the measurements, cut the plywood to match the bed's width. This creates the base of the headboard (we used a 60- × 40-inch sheet of plywood).
3. Using a matte knife, cut the sheet metal to the size of the headboard. (If the sheet metal isn't big enough, cut strips to match the board's width.)
4. Using the staple gun, attach the sheet metal to the headboard, stapling at the edges.
5. Using liquid nails, line the edges of the headboard and attach corner edging (trim if too long).

6. Using a hammer and tacks, attach galvanized patches and duct screens in the desired pattern on the sheet metal. (We used about sixteen patches to cover our headboard.)
7. Screw a hook into the top edge of the headboard 5 inches in from one corner. Repeat for the other corner.
8. Screw two additional hooks into the wall, at the same distance apart as your headboard hooks, making sure you put them at the proper height. (The bottom of your headboard should meet the edge of your bed.)
9. Hang the headboard.

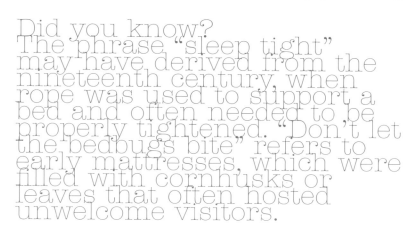

Did you know? The phrase "sleep tight" may have derived from the nineteenth century, when rope was used to support a bed and often needed to be properly tightened. "Don't let the bedbugs bite" refers to early mattresses, which were filled with cornhusks or leaves that often hosted unwelcome visitors.

Elevated

I love the little wooden platters
that sushi is served on—they're
so minimal and modern. I'm not
saying you're a piece of sushi that's
curling up for the night, but I am
saying a platform bed is chic.

Supplies

Standard bed frame
½-inch-thick plywood (enough to fit
over top of the frame)
Wood slats
Sushi mats (enough to cover the
exposed part of the platform)
Wood stain
Nails

Tools

Glue gun and glue sticks
Hammer
Paintbrush
Tape measure

Getting Started

1. Measure the length and width
   of the mattress, adding an extra
   foot onto the length. (This portion
   will be what extends out from
   the mattress.)
2. Using these measurements, cut
   the plywood. (This will be the
   platform.)
3. Place on top of the edge of your
   bed frame.
4. Measure the sides and front
   portion of the platform that
   extends from the frame.
5. Using those measurements, cut
   three wood slats to fit over that
   area of the platform.
6. Stain the platform and slats.
   Let dry.
7. Using hammer and nails, attach
   wood slats to the edges of the
   platform.
8. Measure the exposed area on
   the top of the foot of the platform.
   (This is where the bamboo mats
   will lie.)
9. Cut and stain the number of
   bamboo mats needed to cover
   the top of the plywood that
   extends out from the frame.
   Let dry.
10. Using the glue gun, attach the
    bamboo mats to the top of the
    platform. Let dry.
11. Lay the mattress on top of the
    completed platform.

Make it chic:
There are 1,250 different
species of bamboo, and China
is its largest producer.

Supplies

White comforter, or duvet

Thick decorative ribbon

Thread

Thumbtacks (2)

Fabric glue

Tools

Scissors

Needle

Hammer

Getting Started

1. Spread the duvet out over the bed.
2. Using fabric glue, attach two strips of ribbon on either side down the length of the duvet. Let dry.

Bed Bundle

Remember the agony of having to make your bed every morning when you were a kid? I never quite learned how to get those corners right and instead just threw the comforter sloppily over the sheets. Well, here's a way to give your bed a neat, clean look, a technique that would make any mother proud.

3. To tie the bed bundle into place, secure two strips of ribbon pattern side down, using thumbtacks and hammer, to the end of the bed on either side. Be sure to place the thumbtacks in the center of the fabric to secure them in place. (These strips can be tacked down to your bed frame, your footboard, or the platform on your bed, whichever you have.)
4. Roll the duvet down toward the foot of the bed.
5. Pull the tacked-down strips up and tie them around the circumference of the roll to hold into place.

Here to stay: The term "bedroll" has been used to describe a sleeping bag and also any type of portable bed. But let us not forget our four-legged friends: In their world, "bedroll" refers to a fleece-lined cover used to keep from getting pet hair on furniture.

Silk Roll

We thought this bed needed a bit of pizzazz, something to take it up a notch, and I instantly thought of a bolster pillow. A bolster does exactly what its name suggests—it gives you a lift, a bit of support. It also gives an air of sophistication.

Supplies

2 standard king-size pillows
2 king-size pillowcases
Red silk fabric
Self-adhesive Velcro
Thread
Thick decorative ribbon
Frogs
Fabric glue

Tools

Scissors
Needle
Tape measure

Getting Started

1. Stuff pillowcases with the pillows.
2. With the pillows' openings facing each other, sew the two cases together. (This will create the roll.)
3. Measure the width of the roll and cut three pieces of red fabric—one piece to cover the center of the roll where the pillowcases meet and two pieces to wrap around either side of the roll. (These pieces can be as narrow or as wide as you like. We made our middle piece the boldest and widest.)
4. Using fabric glue or needle and thread, hem the edges of the fabric to prevent fraying.
5. Wrap your fabric tightly around the desired areas on the pillow and secure in the back using self-adhesive Velcro.
6. Using fabric glue, attach three frogs, evenly spaced, on the front of the middle section.
7. Using fabric glue, line the inside edge of the two outer red strips of fabric with contrasting ribbon and the outside edges of the middle red strip as well.

Did you know?
Foreign names for silk include
soie (French), *seide* (German),
seta (Italian), and *seda* (Spanish).

Washboard Shelves

Some people would say washboards are obsolete. Who wants to do laundry the old-fashioned way? So I say saw off the legs, connect them to a few shelves, and show off the shiny ridge pattern in a book-smart way.

Supplies
Wooden washboards (2 per shelf)
Precut wood planks
L brackets with screws
Extra screws

Tools
Drill
Handsaw

Get Started

1. At a lumberyard, have five pine planks cut widthwise to the length of the body of washboard and 4 feet long.
2. Using the handsaw, saw off the legs of the washboards.
3. Lay one plank flat on the floor. Lay one washboard, on its side, on the plank about 2 inches in from one end. (It should be perpendicular to the wooden plank.)
4. Where the washboard and wood plank meet, drill in two L brackets: one toward the front inside corner, one toward the back inside corner. This should secure the washboard.
5. Repeat steps 3 and 4 for the opposite end of the plank, with the second washboard facing the same direction as the first.
6. When both washboards are in place, they should be able to support the next wood plank. Lay the second plank on top of the washboards, lining it up with the first plank underneath.
7. Over one washboard, drive three screws into the surface of the second wood plank; the screws should reach through the plank and into the washboard below it. This should secure the second tier of the shelves to the washboard.
8. Repeat step 7 for the second washboard.
9. Repeat steps 3–8 until the shelving unit is complete.

Did you know? Columbus Washboard Company, founded in 1895, was probably the first commercial manufacturer of washboards. Its number one customers are washboard musicians and people in various Amish communities.

A Meshy Situation

If you thought screens were made just to fit inside a window, here's a way to use them indoors. The result is ultramodern, easy to clean, and inexpensive. Be careful, though— you might wind up keeping the bugs in, instead of out.

Supplies

Gray plastic mesh screen (1 per window)
Thin-gauge metal washers
Thread
3-inch binder rings
Silver metal curtain rod and hardware (1 per window)

Tools

Scissors
Tape measure
Upholstery needle
Screw gun and screws

Getting Started

1. Measure the windows from top of casing to floor and from edge to edge of frame.
2. Cut mesh to match measurements and lay out on a flat surface.
3. Arrange washers in a pattern on the mesh.
4. Using needle and thread, make four stitches through the hole of the washers and attach them to the mesh.
5. Once all the washers are attached, sew on a line of washers evenly across the top edge of the mesh and push the binder rings through the mesh and washer.
6. Attach the curtain rod hardware to either side of the window according to the instructions.
7. String binder rings onto curtain rod and hang.

Rule of thumb: The five standard types of binder rings are circle, D-ring, trapezoid, elliptical, and arch-shaped.

Hanging Hats

Straw hats always seem to have
a brim perfectly sized to shade
out the sun, and everyone looks
so calm and serene when wearing
a straw hat. With this project you
can bring some of that simple
elegance indoors.

Supplies

Chinese straw hat
Two 1-inch galvanized pipes,
3 inches long (they should have
threading on both ends)
Three 1-inch galvanized pipes,
each 6 inches long (they should
have threading on both ends)
Flanges
Lamp sockets
Wall anchor
Cord with plug
Hollow threaded rod
Reducer coupling for threaded rod
Lightbulb
Connector
Elbow joint

Tools

Screw gun and screws
Flathead screwdriver
Scissors

Getting Started

1. Using a connector, screw
   together two pieces of the 3-inch
   galvanized pipe to create one
   long piece.

2. Using the elbow joint, screw this
   long piece to the remaining
   piece of pipe. (This will create
   an L shape.)

3. Attach wall anchor to the long
   end of the L.

4. Cut a small hole at the top of
   the hat and push the end of the
   long galvanized pipe without
   the flange through the hole.

5. Attach the threaded rod to the
   opposite end of the long pipe,
   using a reducer coupling.

6. Push the cord all the way
   through the piping and wall
   anchor, starting from the inside
   of the hat.

7. At the flange end of the
   lamp, attach the plug to the
   electrical wire.

8. At the opposite end of the cord,
   attach the lamp socket, and
   screw it into the end of the
   reducer coupling.

9. Using the screw gun, attach
   the coupling to the wall at the
   preferred height.

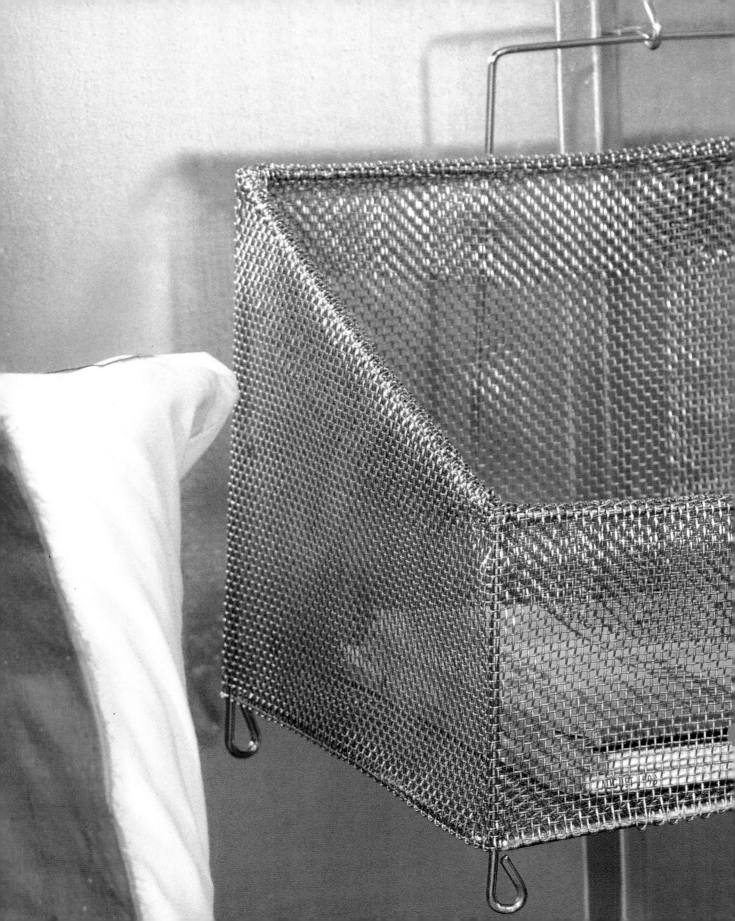

Steel Frame

In this project we took some of the aluminum sheet metal left over from the wall and our headboard and decided to have a little more fun. So we created a picture frame to keep up the clean, sleek look of the room.

Supplies

Aluminum sheet metal (thin gauge)
Plain wood picture frame
Heavy-duty glue
Thumbtacks
Metal washers

Tools

Matte knife
Tape measure

Getting Started

1. Measure the width and the length on all four sides of the frame.
2. Using your measurements, cut four strips of metal that are 1 inch longer and 1 inch wider than the frame.
3. Using metal glue, first attach the two horizontal strips and then the two vertical ones. Let dry.
4. Using thumbtacks, attach a washer to each corner of the frame.

Suspended

My first job was working at a local Dairy Queen. Contrary to what you might think, it was not the ice cream I loved but the french fries. Throughout my shift, they were always at my fingertips. I guess that's when my love affair with the fry basket began. Today I use it as a great place to store a pocketful of necessities, and to daydream about the time when it didn't matter how many french fries I ate.

Supplies

Aluminum deep-fry basket
Silver nails

Tools

Hammer

Getting Started

1. Choose the area on the wall where you want to hang your basket.
2. Using hammer and nails, hang the fry basket from its handle.

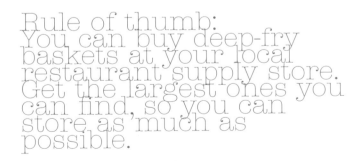

Rule of thumb: You can buy deep-fry baskets at your local restaurant supply store. Get the largest ones you can find, so you can store as much as possible.

LIVING ROOM

Walk the Plank

A little color goes a long way,
so put a little spring back into your
step with the floor under your feet.
Ready, set, paint.

Supplies

Wide precut wood planks
Paint (2 different shades of the
same color and 1 contrasting color
for the stripe)
Masking tape
Wood nails

Tools

Paintbrushes
Ruler
Hammer

Getting Started

1. Measure the floor you want
   to cover and, using those measurements, buy enough precut
   wood planks to cover the floor.
2. Paint planks in alternating shades.
3. Using masking tape, place two
   strips running lengthwise,
   leaving a space between them
   to create the width of the stripe
   you would like to have.
4. Paint the space in between
   the two strips of tape with the
   contrasting color. Let dry.
5. Remove tape.
6. Using hammer and nails, attach
   wood planks side by side in
   place on the floor.

The big idea: As we all know, the term
"walk the plank" refers to a form of
execution, but most people don't know that
walking the plank was used more as a
dramatic device in fiction than in real life.

The Writing on the Wall

One of the things I love about living in an urban environment is the art, which is everywhere. Murals, graffiti, and billboards all add to the stimulation of life in the city. Choose a few symbols or words that mean something to you as a source of inspiration.

Supplies

Rolls of craft paper

Vellum paper

Rolls of tracing paper

Silver paint

Copper nails

Freezer wrap

Decorative wooden beads

Spray adhesive

Tools

Hammer

Paint roller

Tape measure

Scissors

Getting Started

MAKING THE WALLPAPER

1. Measure the height and width of the wall area you are covering.
2. Lay out the craft paper on a flat surface, and cut the paper into strips to match those measurements.
3. Cut strips of tracing paper the same length as the craft paper, but shorten the width 5 inches on each side.
4. Using spray adhesive, attach the strips of tracing paper to the center of the craft paper. Let dry.
5. Cut freezer paper to the same length of the tracing paper, less 2 inches on each side.
6. Using the paint roller, paint the strips of freezer paper silver. Let dry.
7. Using spray adhesive, attach the silver strips to the tracing paper. Let dry.

MAKING THE CALLIGRAPHY

8. Using the computer, print out your symbols, words, or numbers onto vellum paper.
9. Using spray adhesive, attach the vellum squares to the silver strips, spacing them approximately 1 to 2 feet apart.

HANGING THE WALLPAPER

10. Using the decorative wooden beads, hang the paper by hammering copper nails through the beads into the wall. (We hung our beads with nails spaced evenly apart along the edges of the paper.)

Rule of thumb: If you are having a hard time with the longer pieces, you can create the wallpaper in shorter sections; this way, it's easier to work with.

エ

イ

カ

ク

キ

ア

オ

オ

キ

イ

Green, Green Grass

When you live in an urban environment, it's important to stay in touch with nature. With a quick trip to your local nursery, you can bring a little green, green grass into your urban hideaway.

Supplies
Heavy-duty screws
Aluminum stud (same length as the wall you wish to hang it on)
Trays of grass

Tools
Screwdriver
Tape measure

Getting Started
1. Measure desired height for placement of aluminum stud. (We put it at a height where you would normally place a chair rail, about 36 inches up from the floor.)
2. Using the screwdriver, attach the stud to the wall.
3. Take the grass and place it along the inside of the stud.

Rule of thumb: To extend the life of your grass, occasionally spritz it with water from a spray bottle.

Keep it simple: Wheat grass is the most common form of grass sold in trays.

Under Construction

I never seem to have enough
room on my coffee table for all the
candles, books, and magazines—
the clutter is endless. So my
philosophy is: If you want a piece
of furniture that fits your needs,
make it yourself. In this project, you
will be able to fit everything under
the sun within these two tiers.

Supplies

Plywood (2 square pieces, cut to
the desired size)
Rubber wheels
Screws
Sushi mats
Wood stain
Paint
Finishing nails
Aluminum pipe (threaded on both
ends)
Mounts to fit the width of the pipe
Wood corner edging

Tools

Hammer
Screwdriver
Paintbrushes
Tape measure
Glue gun and glue sticks

Getting Started

MAKING THE TIERS

1. Using a glue gun, attach the
   sushi mats to both pieces of
   plywood, covering their entire
   surfaces. (If you find there is
   excess mat hanging off, you can
   trim it with scissors).
2. Using a paintbrush, stain the
   mat-covered squares. Let dry.
3. Measure length and width of
   plywood squares for corner
   edging.
4. Paint the corner edging. Let dry.
5. Using hammer and nails, attach
   corner edging to the sides of the
   plywood squares.
6. Using a screwdriver, attach
   the wheels to the first plywood
   square. (This will be your
   first tier.)

ATTACHING THE TIERS

7. Measure the distance where
   you would like the second tier
   to fit above the first tier.
   (There was 1 foot of space
   between our tiers.)
8. Buy your pipe to size.
9. Using the screwdriver, attach
   a piece of pipe with mount
   attached to each of the four
   corners of the first tier.
10. Center the second tier, face side
    up, over the pipes, then attach
    with a screwdriver.

Yes, you can:
If you don't feel
comfortable drilling
holes into the backs and
sides of your sofa, you
could use velcro to
attach the panels.

Unattached

If you're like me, you want to
change your living room around
every month, constantly searching
for a new look. So here's a great
trick—wheels. Yes, wheels: Not only
do they help out when you don't
have an extra pair of hands, but if
you choose giant industrial-looking
wheels, they can add to the whole
industrial-chic look.

Supplies
Luan
Black vinyl
Rubber wheels (number according
to the number of legs on your
furniture)
Hook and eyes
Screws

Tools
Screwdriver
Glue gun and glue sticks
Tape measure
Scissors

Getting Started

1. Detach the original legs from
   the sofa.
2. Using the screwdriver, attach
   the rubber wheels to the sofa in
   place of the legs.
3. Measure the sides and back of
   the sofa.
4. Cut the luan into three pieces
   according to these measurements:
   one piece for the back and two
   for the sides.
5. Using the measurements of the
   luan, cut the vinyl.
6. Using a glue gun, glue the
   vinyl to the luan.
7. Attach the hooks to the sides
   and back of the sofa.
8. Using a glue gun, attach
   the eyes to the top of the
   vinyl panels.
9. Hang the panels from the
   hooks on the sides and back
   of the sofa.

Screen Star

Here in my workshop, we don't believe in plain old shades and blinds. We always do something that is unique and different, not to mention fun. And we have a winner for you. The best part is that it's on wheels, so you can put these in front of any window where you need to block out a little light, or you can use them to block out the person sitting next to you.

Supplies

Large wood picture frame
Square piece of plywood (large enough to use as a base)
4 metal wheels
6 pipe connectors
Mesh fabric
Paint
Aluminum pipe (four 5-inch pieces that are threaded on both ends)
Metal mounts
Screws

Tools

Paintbrush
Staple gun and staples
Screwdriver
Tape measure
Scissors

Getting Started

1. Paint picture frame and plywood square the same color. Let dry.
2. Using a screwdriver, attach wheels to the bottom of the plywood square base (one in each corner).
3. Take one piece of pipe and attach a mount to one end.
4. Using a screwdriver, attach the pipe with mount attached to the center of the plywood base.
5. Using the pipe connectors, attach the remaining pieces of pipe together to make one long piece that reaches the bottom of the window.
6. Measure and cut the fabric to fit the picture frame.
7. Using a staple gun, staple the fabric to the back of the picture frame.
8. Using a screwdriver, attach a mount to the bottom of the wood frame.
9. Screw the frame onto the pipe on the wood base.

Industrial Strength

To re-create the downtown loft look of exposed pipes, we've created lighting with copper tubing. The industrial style is a nice complement to our Asian-inspired theme.

Supplies

Lighting kit
Copper pipe (the size depends on how tall you want your table lamp to be)
Copper connector
Store-bought paper lantern
Round aluminum electrical base
Mount (the width of the copper pipe)

Tools

Screwdriver

Getting Started

1. Attach the elbow connector to one end of the copper pipe.
2. Thread the electrical cord through the elbow connector and up through the top of the pipe.
3. Attach the plug to the electrical cord on the end that extends from the elbow.
4. Attach the light socket with lightbulb on the opposite end of the pipe.
5. Using a screwdriver, attach the mount to the center of the aluminum electrical base.
6. Screw the bottom of the copper pipe into the mount.
7. Slip the paper lantern over the lightbulb, allowing the hook on the end of the lantern to rest on the lightbulb.

Rule of thumb: Washi, or rice paper, is used to make paper lanterns.

Wok This Way

A lamp made out of a wok?
Who knew?

Supplies

Lighting kit
Large carbon steel wok
Fabric (any fabric, just dark
enough to hide the wire)
2 large metal S hooks
Epoxy
2 pieces of metal chain

Tools

Wire cutters
Tape measure
Needle and thread

Getting Started

1. Using epoxy, attach the lighting
   unit to the inside of the wok,
   directly in the center. Let dry.
2. Slide one S hook onto each
   handle of the wok.
3. Measure and cut enough fabric
   to create a sleeve that will cover
   the chains. (Our chains were
   each 12 inches long.)
4. Using needle and thread, sew
   the side edges of the fabric
   together, creating a tubelike
   shape or sleeve to slide over
   the chains.
5. Attach a chain to each S hook
   on either side of the wok.
6. Thread the wire from the
   lighting unit through the links
   of one chain.
7. Cover the chains with fabric
   sleeves.
8. Connect the two chains with the
   wire that was woven through
   the one chain.
9. Using a ceiling hook attach the
   top link of each chain. Plug in
   the lamp.

The big idea: The wok is an all-purpose Asian pan, resembling a bowl; it is distinguished by its high, sloping sides. The traditional wok is 14 inches in diameter and is made of carbon steel. Woks that have a hammered surface look nice, but hammering does not make for a better wok.

Pillow Perfect

A throw pillow is a great way to
soften the rough industrial look.
The sumptuous silk fabric adds just
the right touch of luxury to this
deconstructed design.

Supplies

Silk fabric
Pillow form
Wide decorative ribbon
Safety pins

Tools

Glue gun and glue sticks
Scissors

Getting Started

1. Spread out the fabric (good side
   down) and place the pillow
   directly on top.
2. Cut enough fabric to cover the
   entire pillow front and back.
3. Wrap the fabric around the
   pillow as if you were wrapping
   a gift.
4. Secure in place with safety pins.
5. Take a strip of wide ribbon and
   wrap it around the middle of
   the pillow. (The fabric or ribbon
   should be wide enough to hide
   the safety pins.)
6. Connect the two ends of the
   ribbon with hot glue.
7. Using another dab of hot glue,
   secure the band in place
   directly above the safety pins.

Nature's Bounty

Orchids are one of my favorite
flowers; they are so simple, yet
so beautiful. That's why this
arrangement is a perfect finishing
touch to any room.

Supplies

1 orchid plant
Sticks of thin bamboo
Potting soil
Limestone rocks
Glass cylinder vase
Alligator clips

Getting Started

1. Put a 3- to 4-inch layer of potting
   soil in the bottom of the vase.
2. Place a 3- to 4-inch layer of
   limestone rocks on top of the
   soil layer.
3. Repeat steps 1 and 2 until there
   are about 4 inches left to the top
   of the vase; this is the space for
   the orchid.
4. Place the orchid (with the moss
   that comes with it) on top of the
   layer of rocks.
5. Using the alligator clips, place a
   stick of bamboo right next to the
   orchid and clip it to the stem of
   the plant.

Yes, you can:
If you can't find
alligator clips in
your local
hardware store,
small binder clips
from an office
supply store will
work too.

My good friend Eric Hughes is solely responsible for this chapter. He has more talent and taste in his little finger than I do in both of my size 8½ feet! He is a big tall man—that is why I call him "Big Tall Eric"—and you'd never think such a giant could be so calm and centered. When I told him I wanted to develop a chapter all about decorating with one color and that I wanted to explore the impact of using only various shades of the same tones, I was thinking bright pink, bold yellow, summery green, perhaps even a shade of plum. But my gentle giant came forward with a much more subtle palette, developing a bedroom of gray and a living room of beige—oh so sophisticated and pure. My book, his colors. Could I? Could I pull back from my lifelong obsession with brightness? Let me back up a bit. It started with the color yellow. When I was growing up, my mom had a tradition: When a daughter turned eleven, she could decorate her own room. Wow! When it was my turn, all I could think was yellow. The only problem was that I didn't have my own room—I shared one with my sister Marlee. And Marlee loved the color blue. How was my debut as a decorator supposed to work? As it stood, I had to ask permission to use the door because it was on Marlee's side of the room. How was I going to decorate a room that wasn't all mine? Half and half, no way! I wanted yellow and lots of it. So my mother came up with a plan. She would give up her sewing room for me. Yes, it was small. Yes, it was in the back of the house. Yes, it was right next to my parents' room. Yes, it was mine. My bright yellow fantasy came true.

Today, I know that I can grow as a businesswoman and an artist only by working with and being influenced by others, especially someone I respect as much as Eric. But I had a hard time with

PICK A COLOR
a one-tone treat

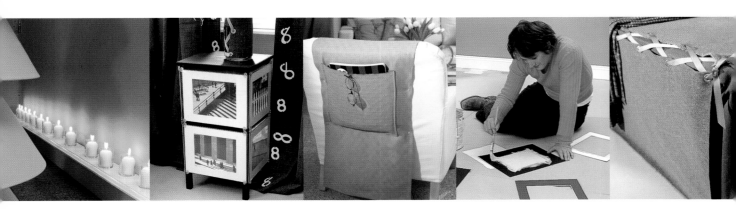

bland colors. My mother always said that the first time you decorate a home, you should play it safe by choosing neutral colors; the second time you can be brave and choose outrageous colors that make you really happy. By selecting the color of dirt we did the opposite of what my mother taught me. Were we not teaching people to play it safe by choosing these monotones? "Trust me," he said, "you will love it.... It is in homage to the artist John Saladino." I didn't have the foggiest idea whom he was referring to, but I nodded my head in acknowledgment. Looking back to my early decorating days, I too had some artistic influences, but they came from the other end of the spectrum: I went through a Picasso blue phase; a Georgia O'Keeffe phase of fresh, bright desert tones; even a Robert Motherwell phase of boldly colored stripes. "Hey, Eric, ever heard of the favorite non-highbrow artist Norman Rockwell?" I don't have Calvin Klein's disciplined love of subtlety. Give me an Isaac Mizrahi circus-color pattern any day! I told myself, *Katie, Katie, remain calm*. Big Tall Eric can be trusted. He will deliver an inspiring environment ... but how?

The day came. Eric's rooms were done. I shut my eyes, held my breath, clenched my teeth, and waited. What is that line in "A Visit from Saint Nicholas"? Oh, yes, "What to my wandering eye did appear ..." Dreamy tans, positively powerful beige, exquisite eggshells, and all lit with the neutral light of border candles. Blah beige does live. Glowing grays, gutsy and gushing heathers all warmed the bedroom. Eric, how much you taught me that day. Subtle tones do have life. Don't get me wrong, I still love my brassy colors, but I do see the light on the other side of the rainbow. So whether you love simple tones or bold, bright colors, embrace just one hue and wrap it all around the room. With just one color, be it loud or quiet, a lasting statement can be made.

As for Eric, rarely does a day go by that I don't thank him for helping the eleven-year-old in me realize the beautiful, centering calmness that can come from the art of subtlety! Think pink, paint the town red, or, like "Big Tall Eric," embrace the drama of earth tones. That's right, I said the drama of earth tones.

BEDROOM

Mat . . . ticulious **floors**

Intersecting Shelves **walls**

Hob Knob **walls**

Head and Shoulders Above the Rest
furniture structure

Tie One On **furniture treatment**

Pillow with a Waistline **furniture treatment**

Bright Lights, Big City **furniture structure**

Crazy Eights **windows**

Pitching Pictures **lighting**

Corset **accessories**

Mat . . . ticulious

One of the things I love about this chapter is its sophistication, which we achieved by using various shades of the same color. This project illustrates that technique with the simple use of paint to transform a floor into a point of interest.

Supplies

3 squares of ready-made 8-ply print museum mats in different sizes, ranging from 4 × 5 inches to 11 × 14 inches.
Semigloss latex (water-based) paint (the same color as your walls)
Semigloss latex paint (in 4 shades contrasting with the wall color)
Polyurethane

Tools

Paintbrushes
Paint roller
Paint tray

Getting Started

1. Paint entire floor evenly in the same color as your walls. Let dry.
2. Starting in the corner of the room, take a mat and place it approximately 4 inches away from the wall.
3. Hold the mat firmly in place.
4. Take one of the four colors and paint a square using the cutout portion of the mat as a stencil. Let dry.
5. Repeat the process, alternating the size and color of the squares along the edges of all four walls in the room, creating a border for your floor. When alternating squares, overlap the edges; this will make a collage-like pattern. Let dry.
6. Apply a coat of polyurethane over the entire floor.

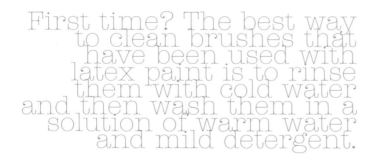

First time? The best way to clean brushes that have been used with latex paint is to rinse them with cold water and then wash them in a solution of warm water and mild detergent.

Intersecting Shelves

I've always been attracted to the precision and clean lines in mazes. These shelves take on that look and add to the streamlined feel of the room.

Supplies
4 hardwood planks (to be used for the shelves)
2 small hardwood planks (to be used to connect the shelving)
Wood stain
Approximately twenty-four 1-inch arched L brackets

Tools
Paintbrush
Screwdriver and screws

Getting Started
CREATING THE SHELVES
1. Using the wood stain, stain all 6 wood planks. Let dry.
2. Using L brackets, connect two shelving planks and one connecting plank together to create a U.
3. Repeat the previous step using the remaining two shelving planks and connecting plank. (This will give you two separate units.)

ATTACHING THE SHELVES
4. Using a screwdriver, attach three additional L brackets, evenly spaced along the length of each shelving plank.
5. Using a screwdriver, attach the first unit to the wall with the open side of the unit facing to the right. (We find that the placement of the shelving unit works best in the top center portion of the wall.)
6. Next attach the second unit with the open side facing left, intersecting the first unit.

Hob Knob

When a room is painted all one color, it becomes small and cozy; however, beware of the fine line between making a room warm and quaint and making it look small and cramped. One way to make this color scheme successful is to draw people's attention up and around a room. That's why we added the architectural detail of a ceiling border. The border adds even more detail because, unlike standard paper borders, it has a third dimension. You don't need those 3-D glasses.

Supplies
Thin flat wooden molding. (This comes in various lengths. Our rooms were 12 × 12 feet, so we chose 6-foot lengths to make the work as easy as possible.)
Round wooden drawer pulls, approximately 1 inch in diameter
Primer
Paint
Wood epoxy
Finishing nails

Tools
Hammer
Paintbrush

Getting Started
1. Attach drawer pulls evenly along molding approximately 6 inches apart using wood epoxy. Let dry.
2. Paint a solid coat of primer over molding and pulls. Let dry.
3. Apply desired paint color. Let dry.
4. Using a hammer and nails, attach molding to the walls approximately 6 inches from the ceiling.
5. If necessary, touch up with additional paint where the seams of the molding meet and where the nails are placed.

Head and Shoulders Above the Rest

As an art history student I always imagined my adult life being full of galleries. That has not been the case, but I have brought the gallery look to this bedroom by hanging picture lights to highlight the headboard covered in the color of choice, gray.

Supplies

½-inch-thick plywood

Batting (enough to cover the plywood)

Fabric (enough to cover the plywood)

Picture light kit with mounting supplies included

Small hook-and-eye kit

Nail with large head

Screws

Tools

Staple gun and staples

Screwdriver

Tape measure

Scissors

Hammer

Getting Started

CREATING THE PANEL

1. Measure and cut plywood to create the headboard. (We had ½-inch plywood cut to the width of the bed and left the length at 6 feet for a nice elongated effect.)

2. Measure and cut the batting to fit the width and height of the headboard, allowing approximately one extra inch on all sides for easier attachment.

3. Cover the front side of the headboard with batting and, using the staple gun, attach it to the back of the headboard.

4. Using the fabric, cover the headboard and batting and again staple along the back of the headboard.

5. Trim the excess fabric.

ATTACHING THE LIGHT

6. Using a screwdriver, attach the picture light to the top center of the headboard.

7. Place the picture light switch at the edge of the headboard and, using a hammer, attach a nail with a large head to the side edge of the headboard.

8. Wrap the cord around the nail head to keep it in place so that you can easily turn the lamp on and off.

SECURING THE HEADBOARD

9. Place the headboard at the head of the bed.

10. Attach the hook from the hook-and-eye kit to the top edge of the headboard.

11. On the wall attach the eye; hook the headboard in place. (Remember, you are not hanging the headboard, just holding it in place.)

Tie One On

Duvets give a comforting, casual look to your bed, but to give it a more formal look, try this project on for size.

Supplies
Fabric
Grosgrain ribbon
Fabric glue

Tools
Grommet kit
Scissors
Tape measure

Getting Started

1. Measure the length and width of the bed, and measure the two sides and the foot of the bed to the floor.
2. Using these measurements, cut the fabric into four panels: one for the top part of the bed, two for the sides, and one for the foot of the bed. Cut 1 inch more than you need on all sides of each panel, so that you have enough to create a hem.
3. Hem unfinished edges, using fabric glue. Let dry.
4. Following the directions on the grommet kit, place grommets approximately 10 inches apart along the three sides of the panel that fits on top of the bed, leaving only the head of the bed grommetless.
5. Repeat this process with the three other panels, but grommet only the top edge of the remaining panels. Make sure the grommets line up with the grommets on the top panel.
6. Lace the ribbon through the grommets shoelace style, attaching all four panels together, knotting at the ends.

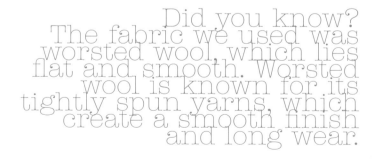

Did you know? The fabric we used was worsted wool, which lies flat and smooth. Worsted wool is known for its tightly spun yarns, which create a smooth finish and long wear.

Pillow with a Waistline

This project was inspired by a great passion of mine, period films. Think of a Victorian lady changing into her evening gown, with her maid pulling her corset oh so tight. This was my way of bringing that period look into the world of decorating.

Supplies

Foam bolster pillow
Fabric
Grosgrain ribbon
Spray adhesive
Fabric glue
Grommet kit

Tools

Scissors
Tape measure

Getting Started

COVERING THE ENDS

1. Measure and cut two circular pieces of fabric to fit the ends of the pillow, 2 inches wider than the diameter.
2. Cut six slits approximately 2 inches deep in equal increments around the circle. (Our pillows were 10 inches in diameter and 12 inches long.)
3. Using spray adhesive, spray the ends of the pillows.
4. Attach one circular piece to one end of the pillow and fold over the fabric in between the slits.

COVERING THE MIDDLE

5. Measure and cut a third piece of fabric to fit around the body of the pillow.
6. Using spray adhesive, spray the remaining area of the pillow.
7. Lay the third piece of fabric flat and roll the pillow over it until the whole pillow is covered.

CREATING THE CORSET

8. Measure a fourth piece of fabric: It should be the same length as the pillow but about 5 inches smaller than its circumference. (You want to have an opening down the center of the pillow to show off your lacing.)
9. Add an extra inch on all sides to create hems. Cut.
10. Using fabric glue, make a 1-inch hem all the way around the edge of the fabric. Let dry.
11. Using the grommet kit, place the grommets approximately 7 inches apart down the length of the corset.
12. Put the corset into place around the bolster pillow.
13. Lace the ribbon through the grommets shoelace style, tighten, and knot.

Did you know? Shoelaces emerged in the 1600s and became a fad.

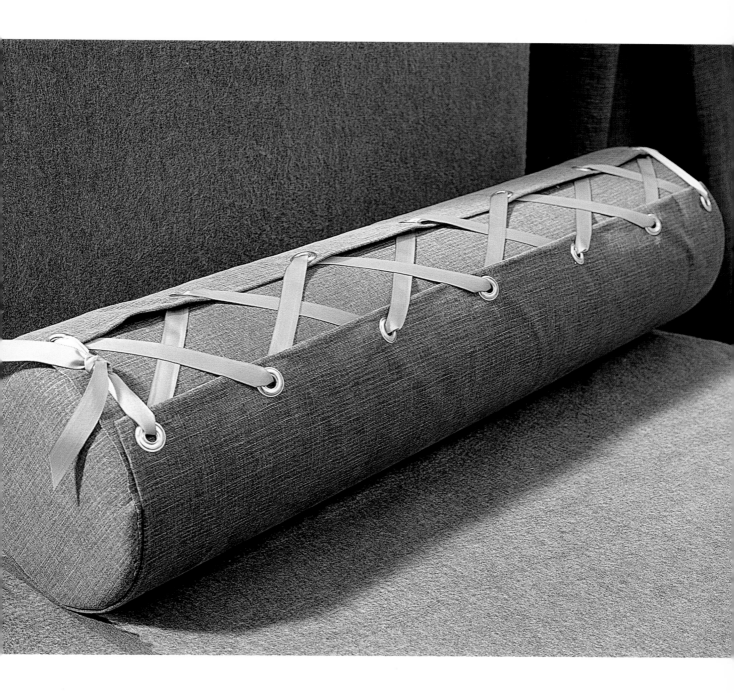

Bright Lights, Big City

There is always something inviting about a city skyline, so the photos chosen for this project have an urban feel to them. It's a friendly reminder all year long that the city is always there when you are ready to explore.

Supplies

Unfinished wood two-tier end table

12 precut Plexiglas panes (wide enough to fit between the legs of the end table)

6 precut picture mats (wide enough to fit between the legs of the end table)

6 black-and-white photos

Plastic mirror brackets (4 per photo)

Wood stain

Basic light fixture

1 sheet black mat board

Self-adhesive Velcro

Screws

Tape

Nuts

Tools

Rag

Drill

Screwdriver

Tape measure

Getting Started

ATTACHING THE LIGHT FIXTURE

1. Using a drill, make a hole in the bottom shelf of the end table. The hole has to be large enough to fit the light fixture through it.
2. Using a rag, apply an even coat of stain over the entire table. Let dry.
3. Screw in light fixture. Secure bottom and top with a nut.

ATTACHING THE FRAMES

4. On a flat surface, tape the black-and-white photo to the museum mat. (If the picture mats are a bit wide, use a utility knife to trim them down.)
5. Holding the matted photo between the legs of the table, mark the spot where brackets need to be in order to hang your frame.
6. Place your matted photo in between two pieces of Plexiglas and secure in place using mirror brackets. Repeat steps 4–6 for the other black-and-white photos, and hang them around the three sides of the table.
7. Measure and cut a piece of black mat board to cover the fourth side of the table and use self-adhesive Velcro to attach.

Basic 123: Resist using fluorescent bulbs in your picture lights—they may cause fading. Standard household bulbs will work fine. For safety's sake, use a low-wattage bulb.

Crazy Eights

Do you have a lucky number? If you love it so much that you have to surround yourself with it all the time, this is a project for you. Take your favorite number and give your boring old draperies a hip new look. Not only will the sight of your favorite number make you happy, but the repetition adds a more modern look to the room. (Think Andy Warhol.)

Supplies

Plastic address numbers in different shapes and sizes (quantity will vary, depending on the size of the draperies)
Yarn (same color as the draperies)
Spray paint
Draperies (solid color)
Drapery rods

Tools

Upholstery needle
Scissors

Getting Started

1. Hang two drapery panels from the desired curtain rod.
2. Using spray paint, spray an even coat on the numbers. Let dry.
3. Using the upholstery needle and yarn, attach the numbers down the left side of each drapery panel.

Pitching Pictures

Again, we've looked to our favorite galleries for inspiration. Take your most cherished photo and display it as if it were a great work of art by giving it a little dimension and illumination.

Supplies

Photograph
1 precut 8-ply museum print mat to fit photo
2 precut Plexiglas the same size as mat
U-shaped plumbing bracket (3-sided, approximately 4 inches square)
Basic light fixture
Several medium binder clips
Screws
Glue
Scotch tape

Tools

Screwdriver

Getting Started

1. Using glue, attach your light fixture to the bottom of the inside of the U-shaped bracket.
2. Using the screwdriver, mount the bracket on the wall.
3. Tape the photo to the print mat.
4. Place the Plexiglas on the back of the print mat.
5. Place another piece of Plexiglas on the front of the print mat.
6. Using a few binder clips, clip the mat with photo and Plexiglas together at the top.
7. At the bottom of the clipped photo, slide the front arm of the bracket in between the Plexiglas and the mat. Put two more binder clips at the bottom of the photo to hold everything in place.

Corset

Like any great director, a decorator
should keep referring to his or her
original theme. So we have dressed
up a vase with another variation of
the corset.

Supplies

Vase with a smooth surface
Fabric (enough to cover the vase)
Fabric glue
Spray adhesive
Grosgrain ribbon

Tools

Grommet kit
Scissors
Tape measure

Getting Started

1. Measure and cut enough fabric
   to wrap around the body of the
   vase, minus about 3 inches.
   (You want to have the vase
   showing, but also leave enough
   fabric for a hem on all sides of
   the panel.)
2. Using the fabric glue, create a
   ½- to 1-inch hem around all the
   edges of the panel. Let dry.
3. Using the grommet kit, attach
   grommets along the edges of
   both ends of the fabric. Line
   your grommets up in matching
   places on either side of the panel.
4. Using the spray adhesive, spray
   the underside of the fabric and
   attach to the body of the vase.
   Be sure to smooth out any
   wrinkles on the fabric before
   the adhesive dries.
5. Lace the ribbon through the
   grommets shoelace style,
   starting with the grommets on
   the bottom of the vase and
   knotting at the top.

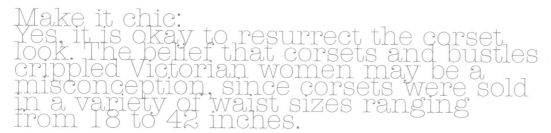

Make it chic:
Yes, it is okay to resurrect the corset
look. The belief that corsets and bustles
crippled Victorian women may be a
misconception, since corsets were sold
in a variety of waist sizes ranging
from 18 to 42 inches.

LIVING ROOM

Corked

When I was a kid, the teacher's pet always got to design the bulletin board. I was never the teacher's pet, so I guess this project serves as my secret revenge—an entire floor with no decorations, just the beautiful color and texture of pure cork. It's enough to drive any teacher's pet crazy.

Supplies

Precut cork tiles
Floor glue
Satin-finish polyurethane

Tools

Paintbrush
Utility knife

Getting Started

1. Lay all the cork tiles in place, starting in the back corner of the room and working toward the front.
2. If the tiles in the last line don't fit evenly with your wall, trim them with a utility knife.
3. Using floor glue, secure the tiles in place. Let adhesive dry.
4. Using a paintbrush, cover the tiles with an even coat of polyurethane. Let dry.

Shelf Life

A shelf often holds the drama of life—displaying books, photographs, and other mementos. But what is more dramatic than a shelf full of candles?

Supplies

4- × ¾-inch wood planks cut to fit the length of the walls
Chair molding (3 inches wide) cut to the same length as the planks
L brackets (½ inch deep and 2 inches wide)
Votive candles and holders
Paint
Screws

Tools

Screwdriver
Paintbrush
Tape measure

Getting Started

1. Measure the four walls of the room and cut the plywood and chair molding accordingly. Remember, two pieces should be cut 3 inches shorter so that they can meet and be flush.
2. Paint the baseboards and chair molding. Let dry.
3. Attach the chair molding to the baseboards using the L brackets. (The molding is what gives the "shelf" look.)
4. Using a screwdriver, attach the baseboards along the bottom of all four walls.
5. Place votive candles along the shelf and light them for a great evening glow.

Here to stay:
Votive candles were originally used for prayer; they might symbolize a wish or desire, or gratitude.

Get Hinged

When I was growing up, I loved magic shows, card tricks, and disappearing acts. I would sometimes find out the trickery behind the magic, but I could never seem to pull the tricks off myself. When it comes to decorating, though, I am proud to say I am capable of creating whimsical illusions. For instance, the placement of these hinges gives the appearance that the room is able to fold right up.

Supplies
12 hinges (4 inches
or larger)
Screws

Tools
Screwdriver

Getting Started
1. Using a screwdriver, place three hinges along the walls in one corner of the room at 2-foot intervals.
2. Repeat step 1 in all four corners of the room.

Keep it simple:
A dab of hot glue
on the backs of
the hinges will
hold them in
place long
enough to get
the screws in.

Screening Room

A great way to give attention to a simple couch is to give it height and surround it with elegant fabric. To achieve this, I've adapted one of my favorite objects—the screen.

Supplies

3 panels of plywood (¾ inch thick)
Enough fabric to cover all three panels
Grosgrain ribbon
Upholstery tacks
Hinges
Screws

Tools

Staple gun and staples
Hammer
Screwdriver
Tape measure
Scissors

Getting Started

1. Measure the plywood and cut it into three panels to fit around the sofa. The side panels should extend beyond the arms of the couch about 8 inches, and the back panel should be 1–2 inches wider than the back of the sofa. All three pieces should be approximately 5 inches taller than the height of the back of the couch.

2. Cut a piece of fabric large enough to cover one plywood panel piece. (Think of the fabric measurement as you would think of a piece of gift wrap used to cover a box.)

3. Wrap the piece of fabric all the way around the panel. Make the two ends of the fabric meet at the bottom edge of the plywood panel. Secure the two pieces together by using a staple gun and stapling the fabric into the bottom edge of the plywood panel.

4. Trim and fold the two sides of the fabric just as you would if you were gift-wrapping the sides of a box, making the two ends of the fabric meet at the side edge of the plywood panel. Secure the two pieces together by using a staple gun and stapling the fabric into the side edge.

5. Repeat step 4 on the other side of the panel.

6. To finish the side panels of the screen, place a strip of ribbon along the edges of the panels and nail down, using upholstery tacks approximately 5 inches apart from each other.

7. Using the hinges, attach the three panels to create a screen. Make sure you sandwich the center panel in between the two side panels, leaving the two trimmed edges exposed. Space the hinges evenly, approximately 8 inches apart. Use a screwdriver and screws to secure the hinges.

You can't go wrong:
The main advantage of plywood is its even
distribution of strength and stiffness.

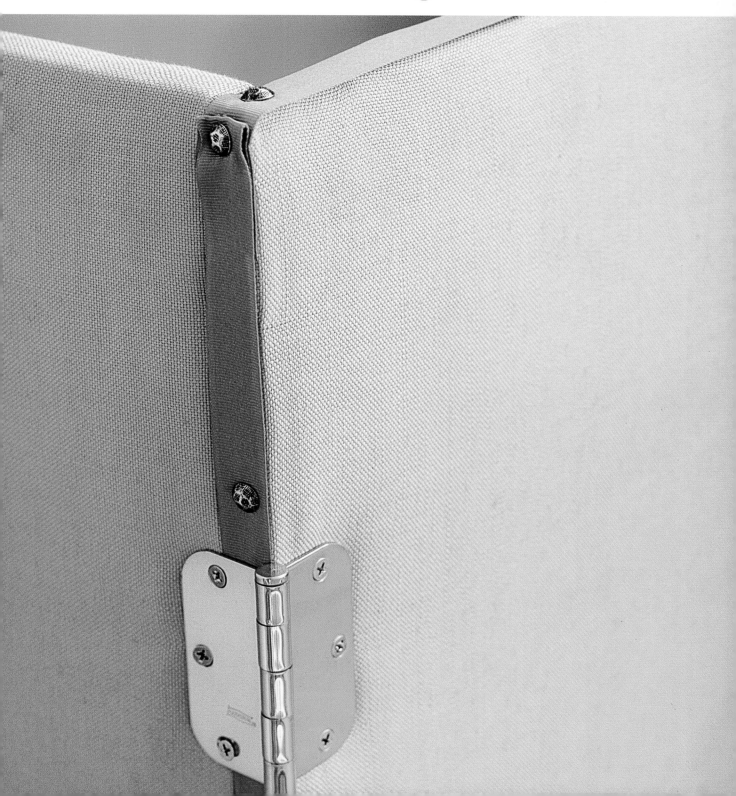

Check Your Pockets

Table runners add detail to a tabletop as well as protection for the surface, so why not apply them to chairs?

Supplies
Fabric
Fabric glue

Tools
Ruler
Tape measure
Scissors

Getting Started

CREATING THE RUNNER

1. Remove cushions from the chair.
2. Measure the chair at its narrowest. Then measure its length, starting with the front of the seat of the chair and going up over the back of the chair and down to the floor.
3. Cut the fabric to your measurements, leaving ½ inch extra on all sides for a hem.
4. To create a hem, fold over ½ inch of fabric around all four sides of your runner and use fabric glue to hold it in place.

CREATING THE POCKET

5. Place the runner on the chair to gauge where the pocket should go. The pocket should lie approximately 8 inches down from the top of the chair and 4 inches in from either side.
6. Keeping these measurements in mind, use a ruler to determine the size of the pocket (including 1 inch excess fabric to allow for room in your pocket and an additional ½ inch extra on all sides for a hem).
7. Using your measurements, trace the shape and size of the pocket onto the fabric with a pen.
8. Cut fabric.
9. Create a finished edge all the way around the pocket by folding over ½ inch of the fabric on all four sides and use fabric glue to hold in place.
10. Attach the pocket to the runner and secure it in place by using fabric glue along the two sides and bottom edge of the pocket.
11. Place runner on chair.
12. Place the seat cushions back on the chair. They will help hold the runner in place.

Rough Rider

When you think of sandpaper, "warm" and "homey" are probably not the first words that come to mind. However, in this project I am attempting to change sandpaper's rough reputation.

Supplies
Coffee table
Sandpaper (in different colors and textures)
Spray adhesive

Tools
Utility knife
Straightedge
Tape measure

Getting Started
CREATING THE TABLETOP

1. Lay out the sandpaper to create a pattern that will work best with the coffee table.
2. Using a utility knife and straightedge, cut the sandpaper to the appropriate sizes needed to cover the coffee table.
3. Using the spray adhesive, spray the backs of the sandpaper pieces and apply pieces to the table. (The adhesive dries fairly quickly, so adjust imperfections right away.)

COVERING THE SIDES AND LEGS

4. Holding up the sandpaper to one side of a table leg, trace as much of its width and length onto the back of the sandpaper as can easily fit.
5. Using a utility knife, cut out the piece.
6. Continue tracing and cutting out pieces until all four sides of the leg are covered. (It is as if you are cutting out and putting together pieces of a puzzle that will create a pattern covering the entire leg.)
7. Using spray adhesive, secure sandpaper pieces to the table leg.
8. Repeat steps 4 through 7 on the remaining legs and sides of the table.
9. If you like, place glass on top to finish it off.

Keep it simple: The top of the table will usually accommodate whole sheets of sandpaper, whereas the sides and legs require a bit of detail work. This is one reason to cover only the tabletop.

Trim by Dom

I used cork in this project, not only because it repeats the texture on the floor but because I am a sucker for a decorative bottle of wine or champagne. Since the cork is the ornament at the top of many beautiful bottles, I thought corks could also be used to dress up simple curtain panels.

Supplies

Bottle corks (enough to line the edge of 2 curtain panels)
Small eye hooks (1 per cork)
Decorative trim
Yarn
Thread
2 panels of draperies for each window
Curtain rings

Tools

Upholstery needle
Sewing needle
Scissors
Tape measure

Getting Started

1. Screw one eye hook, into the center of the small end of each cork.

2. Measure and cut enough trim to hang along the outer edges of the draperies.

3. Using an upholstery needle and yarn, attach the corks to the trim, spacing them approximately 1 to 2 inches apart along the trim.

4. Using the upholstery needle and yarn, attach the trim at four places along the outer edges of the drapes.

5. Using a needle and thread, attach round curtain rings to the top of each curtain panel.

6. Hang the curtain panels.

You can't go wrong. Mixing new corks, old cork stoppers, and wine bottle corks will create a fun look.

Boxed In

In this room, my drapery rod needed a finished look but all the prefab, premolded, preexisting drapery ends seemed trite. I needed something more modern, geometric, and simple. Aha! A box. It's square, it's different, it's modern!

Supplies

Precut wood dowels (1 for each window)
Paint
Plain paper boxes with lids (2 for each curtain rod)
Washer and screw (2 per rod)
Double-stick tape

Tools

Screwdriver
Awl
Paintbrush

Getting Started

1. Paint the wood dowels. Let dry.
2. Using an awl, puncture a small hole in the center of the bottom of the box.
3. Place a screw with a washer through the hole and, using a screwdriver, screw the box into the end of the wood dowel, bottom end first.
4. Repeat process on other end of wood dowel.
5. Place lids on both boxes.
6. Keep the lids from falling off by applying a piece of double-stick tape between the lid and the box.

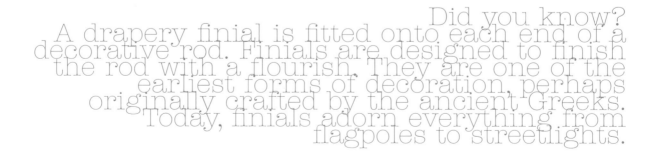

Did you know? A drapery finial is fitted onto each end of a decorative rod. Finials are designed to finish the rod with a flourish. They are one of the earliest forms of decoration, perhaps originally crafted by the ancient Greeks. Today, finials adorn everything from flagpoles to streetlights.

Shades of Light

Here is a little brain teaser for you, a lamp made entirely out of lampshades.

Supplies

5 lampshades (all the same size and color)
36 inches of threaded rod
Threaded bracket
Nuts to fit width of the rod
Plywood (cut to approximately 2 inches smaller than the largest circumference of the lampshade)
Screws
Basic light fixture with harp
Lightbulb

Tools

Screwdriver

Getting Started

ASSEMBLING THE LAMP

1. Cut a small piece of plywood to act as your base (it should be small enough to hide under the lampshade).
2. Using a screwdriver and two screws, attach the threaded rod bracket to the plywood.
3. Screw the threaded rod into the bracket.
4. Using the threaded rod, thread a nut down to where the first lampshade will sit (the first lampshade should be just off the ground, hiding the plywood base).
5. Attach the first lampshade.
6. Thread another nut down to secure the lampshade in place. (Screw the top and bottom nuts together, sandwiching the lampshade securely in place. Do it now because this is hard to do once the entire lamp is assembled.)
7. Repeat steps 4–6 using three more shades. (Make sure the shades are placed approximately 3 inches apart; this will create an overlap.)

LIGHTING

8. Assemble basic light fixture with harp.
9. Screw the bottom of the light fixture onto the top of the threaded rod.
10. Slide the harp onto the light fixture and place the final lampshade on top of the harp.

Tightly Wound

Maybe in time scientists will discover that vases can sense the weather. Here at the workshop we are way ahead of them.

Supplies
Vase, preferably square
Fabric
Grosgrain ribbon
Fabric glue

Tools
Scissors
Tape measure

Getting Started

1. Measure and cut fabric to fit around the body of the vase. Keep in mind that the vase should not be completely covered. The fabric should start about 2 inches from the top and bottom of the vase. Leave about 2 inches along the length of the vase uncovered as well.
2. Fold over ½ inch of fabric along all edges, and secure hem with glue. Let dry.
3. Cut four strips of ribbon, each about 4 inches in length.
4. Using fabric glue, attach two ribbons on each side of the fabric, directly across from each other. They should be placed 2 inches in from the edge.
5. Wrap fabric around the vase and knot ribbons.

Getting Started

1. Measure and cut a piece of
   fabric large enough to wrap
   around a pillow, leaving
   enough fabric to create a
   ½-inch hem on all four sides
   and long enough to create a
   15-inch flap.
2. Using fabric glue, fold down a
   ½-inch hem around all four
   sides and hold it in place.
3. Lay the piece of fabric flat,
   hem meeting hem, and fold
   over, leaving 15 inches at the
   top to act as a flap (think of this
   as creating an envelope).
4. Glue the two side edges
   together.
5. Fold over the flap and attach
   to the outside of the flap
   (with fabric glue) six strips of
   grosgrain ribbon (each about
   5 inches in length), three on
   each side, directly opposite
   each other. (Space the ribbon
   strips fairly evenly apart.)
6. Stuff the fabric envelope with
   the pillow, and tie the flap shut.

Fold, Flap, Tie

I'm not much of a game player.
Trust me, you do not want me on
your team for Scrabble or Trivial
Pursuit. However, when it comes to
ticktacktoe, I'm rarely beaten.
The simple assembly of this pillow
reminds me of the simple game
I have mastered.

Supplies

Fabric
Grosgrain ribbon
Pillow
Fabric glue

Tools

Scissors

CABIN FEVER
a walk in the woods

My mom has always said that families are like mobiles: relationships are very delicately balanced, and memories are the strings that hold them together. My grandparents must have known of this analogy, because their stone cottage on Marquette, an island off Michigan, was a place of many happy memories. It was there that all my cousins, aunts, uncles, sisters, and brothers gathered and spent time together.

Flashback to 1975: It was the summer of *Jaws*. I knew Lake Michigan was freshwater, but I was still convinced that a great white could make its way through the Saint Lawrence Seaway to our dock. To me, water skiing no longer seemed like fun. But my dad was determined to rid me of my fright. He insisted on pulling me behind the Chriscraft. I held my breath the whole time, my imagination getting the best of me: *Wait, what is happening?, the boat is slowing down, I'm sinking, my legs are exposed, and at any moment I could be in the belly of a lake shark!* He cut the engine. Panic had set in. I screamed "Dad, what are you doing"? I began to breathe harder, faster. My dad giggled—he was getting quite a kick out of his prank. Soon he smiled and started the boat, and I resumed my afternoon ski. I landed at the dock with both legs intact. He then gave me a geography lesson, proving that it was impossible for any man-eating beast to arrive at our house. I had to admit it made good sense. *Life was fine.*

Flashback to the late 1970s: The years between ages 12 and 16 were not my favorite. I felt awkward

and out of place as I watched my very groovy, terminally cool cousin Mari get dressed in perfectly faded Levis and some exquisitely chosen T-shirt. I felt inadequate as I watched my cousin Ally and my sister Lynn completely restore the engine on their beat-up but oh so fantastic boat, called *The Fraud*. I felt doomed as I listened to my cousin John recite a poem in French, knowing I had just barely learned to spell my middle name. How could my cousin Stephan replace the entire roof by himself? But then Uncle Bruce would arrive. Just the sight of him would fill me with hope and pride. I knew that soon after he arrived he would pull me aside, set me on his knee, pull out a pen and piece of paper, and begin drawing caricatures of everyone and everything that surrounded us—my father with a potbelly, my aunt stubbing her toe. No, Uncle Bruce could not come into the living room just yet, he was creating a cartoon with *me*. How special he made me feel. *I was okay.*

Flashback to any summer: When Uncle Moses, better known, as Moey, walked up the path, every child would scurry. We knew that if our eyes met his, within moments we would be chopping and stacking wood, cutting grass, digging a garden, weeding the beach—doing hard manual labor usually assigned to prison inmates. Without fail, though, the moment would come. All would dutifully listen to instructions and set off to complete their tasks. There was no talking, no negotiating, no questioning of Moses's orders. (His biblical name suited him well.) I will never say my uncle Moey was carefree, but I will say that seeing a smile break across his face at the sight of a job well done was one of my most satisfying experiences. The way his stern eyes would sparkle when the boathouse was swept and tidy made me realize his regard for our property. It made me realize his devotion to keeping the family whole. *The world was right.*

My grandparents must have known how important surroundings are to a family, or they would never have bothered with this rustic cabin in the woods. Flags hung on the wall, vintage rifles served as frames for old maps, hollowed-out logs were used for flower vases, and all couches were revered for their comfort. The style was a comfortable casual that celebrated all the things in the surrounding woods—forest greens, mellow tree-trunk browns, and dusty blues filled the rooms.

BEDROOM

Hide-and-Sleek

If you cannot find a rug that works
for you, make one. And if you can't
afford leather, how about pleather?

Supplies

3 colors of pleather (2 yards of
each)
Leather cord

Tools

Awl
Fabric scissors
Large upholstery needle
Tape measure

Getting Started

1. Cut one 2- × 4-foot rectangle
   from each of three colors
   of pleather.
2. Cut one 2-foot-square piece
   from each color.
3. Lay the three rectangles on the
   floor.
4. Lay one square at the end of
   each rectangle.
5. Using the awl, punch holes 1
   inch apart and 1 inch in from
   the edge on the ends where the
   square and the rectangle meet.
6. With the upholstery needle and
   leather cord, stitch the squares
   and rectangles together, forming
   three separate strips. (When
   your leather cord runs out, tie it
   into a double knot on the surface of the rug and start again
   where you left off. This detail
   gives the rug a nice rustic look.)
7. Lay the three strips so that the
   squares are on opposite ends,
   forming a patchwork-type
   pattern.
8. Using the awl, punch holes
   1 inch apart and 1 inch in from
   the edge on the side where
   the strips meet.
9. With the upholstery needle
   and leather cord, stitch the
   strips together lengthwise to
   form a square.

Home Sweet Home

This project is a great way to turn a plain wall into a cabin wall.

Supplies

1- × 6-inch pine planks (enough to cover wall horizontally)
White caulking
Wall screws

Tools

Drill
Caulking gun

Getting Started

1. Place one pine plank horizontally on the wall 3 inches down from the ceiling.
2. Using a drill, screw pine plank into the wall.
3. Continue adding planks until one horizontal layer is complete.
4. Leaving 2½ inches between planks, start your second layer. Continue steps 2–3 until the entire wall is covered.
5. With a caulking gun, squirt the white caulking into the grooves between the pine planks. (Allow the natural roughness to remain, adding to the rustic look.) Let dry.

You can't go wrong: Andrew Jackson, James Polk, James Buchanan, Abraham Lincoln, and James Garfield all proudly claimed to have been born in log cabins.

Rule of thumb: Stretcher bars can be purchased at an art supply store. Ask for the wooden bars painters use to create a canvas.

Strap Me In

I have always been a great fan of all things Hermès. But who's got that much cash? So I've taken their signature equestrian look and made it work on a budget.

Supplies

16 belts
Artist stretcher bars: 6 equal to the width of the bed, 2 equal to the desired height of the baseboard, 2 equal to the desired height of the headboard
Stain
Nuts and bolts

Tools

Staple gun and staples
Drill
Screwdriver
Tape measure
Rags

Getting Started

CREATING THE FRAMES

1. Determine the height of the baseboard by adding 1½ feet to the measurement from the floor to the top of the mattress. Determine the height of the headboard by adding 3 feet to the same measurement.
2. Using two stretcher bars the width of the bed, and two the height of the baseboard, create a frame for the baseboard.
3. Secure the frame by stapling the bars together at all four corners on the back.
4. Repeat steps 1–3 for the headboard frame.
5. To determine the placement of a crossbar, measure the length of a buckled belt.
6. Using this measurement, attach bar parallel to the top edge of the frame. Secure with a staple gun.
7. Using a rag, rub the entire frame with stain. Let dry.

ATTACHING THE BELTS

8. Wrap one belt around the top of the frame and the crossbar. Buckle it.
9. Repeat this step four times, positioning the belts approximately 10 inches from each other.
10. Create a long belt rope by buckling four belts to each other.
11. Weave the belt rope in and out of the vertical belts. When the belt rope meets itself again, buckle it tightly.
12. Repeat steps 2–12 for the headboard.

ATTACHING THE BED FRAMES

13. To attach the baseboard and headboard to the metal bed frame, drill a hole in the stretcher bars where it will line up with the holes on the metal frame. Screw the stretcher bars to the bed frame.

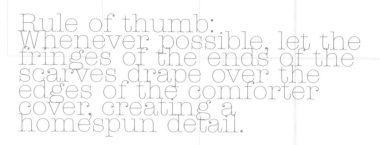

Rule of thumb: Whenever possible, let the fringes of the ends of the scarves drape over the edges of the comforter cover, creating a homespun detail.

Mad About Plaid

Vintage quilts are one of my favorite things to lay across a bed, but they are about as easy to obtain as a cabin in the woods. So why not improvise with a collection of scarves and a simple duvet cover?

Supplies
Comforter (duvet) cover
Wool scarves
Yarn

Tools
Needle
Straight pins
Scissors

Getting Started

1. Lay the scarves flat over the comforter cover, creating a quilted pattern by weaving and overlapping them horizontally and vertically.
2. Using straight pins, pin scarves in place.
3. Using a needle and yarn, connect the scarves to the cover at various points by sewing through the scarf and through only the top sheet of the cover, tying the stitch off in a simple decorative bow.
4. Remove pins.

Tucked Inn

To me, a bed is not fully dressed unless it has a skirt. But I am terminally bored with the selection available, so I have taken matters into my own hands. Think custom-made and think theme, and you will enhance the look of the room.

Supplies
Thick fabric (enough to fit the skirt of the bed)
Self-adhesive Velcro
Fabric glue

Tools
Scissors
Tape measure

Getting Started

1. Remove mattress from bed.
2. Measure the length of the box spring and add 4 inches (for side hems). Measure from the top of the box spring to the floor, adding 10 inches for placing skirt under mattress and for a hem.
3. Cut two equal side panels using this measurement.
4. Repeat steps 1 and 2 for the foot of the bed to create a third panel.
5. Using fabric glue, fold a 2-inch hem along the sides and bottom of the fabric.
6. Lengthwise, tuck the excess 8 inches of fabric under the mattress.
7. Velcro the fabric to the top of the box spring.
8. Repeat steps 1–3 for all sides of the bed.

Buckle Up

To keep that Hermès look going, here's a nightstand to complement the entire room.

Supplies

Leather belts
Square end table
Finishing nails

Tools

Hammer
Scissors

Getting Started

1. Cut a belt long enough to fit across the width of the surface of your end table, adding enough to wrap under the lip of the table at both ends.
2. Cut enough belts to this length to cover the surface of the table, lying side by side.
3. Starting with one belt, place and nail its end to the underside lip on one side of the table. Repeat until the entire side is done.
4. Nail the opposite ends of these belts under the opposite table lip.
5. Repeat steps 1–3 for the adjacent side of the table, creating a second set of straps.
6. Weave the second set of straps under and over the first set. Alternate the beginning weave (first one over, second one under, etc.) until the whole surface of the table is done.
7. Nail the remaining ends of the straps under the lip of the table.

Rule of thumb: The belts will naturally loosen to accept the weave above and below them. Although it might take some patience, the tighter the weave, the better the outcome. The belts will loosen again when they settle.

The Tin Man

Who doesn't daydream about making an entrance into an old, smoky saloon through the swinging doors? With this project, you can do it every time you open and close your windows.

Supplies

½-inch-thick plywood (cut to cover the window frame)
2 sheets of tin roofing (cut approximately the size of the plywood)
Triangle hinges (2 per window)
Silver door handle (1 per window)
Stain
½-inch silver nails
Screws
Nuts and bolts
Marker

Tools

Rags
Hammer
Drill
Screwdriver
Tape measure

Getting Started

CREATING THE SHUTTER

1. With a rag, rub stain on both sides of the plywood. Let dry.
2. Lay one sheet of tin roofing over the plywood.
3. Using ½-inch silver nails, nail the corners and edges of the tin roofing to the plywood.
4. Repeat steps 2 and 3 on the other side of the plywood.
5. Screw on the door handle about 6 inches in from the edge of the shutter, about ⅓ of the way down from the top edge.

ATTACHING THE SHUTTER TO THE WALL

6. Position two hinges on the edge of the shutter opposite the door handle, approximately 6 inches from the top and bottom. Mark on the tin where the holes in the hinges are.
7. On these marks, drill holes all the way through both sheets of tin and plywood.
8. Push the bolts through and screw on the nuts, securing the hinge to the shutter.
9. Center the shutter on the window and screw hinges in place.

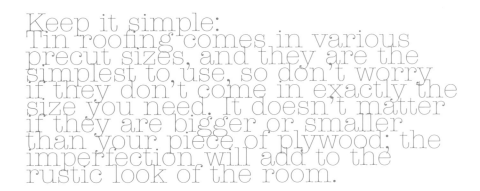

Keep it simple: Tin roofing comes in various precut sizes, and they are the simplest to use, so don't worry if they don't come in exactly the size you need. It doesn't matter if they are bigger or smaller than your piece of plywood; the imperfection will add to the rustic look of the room.

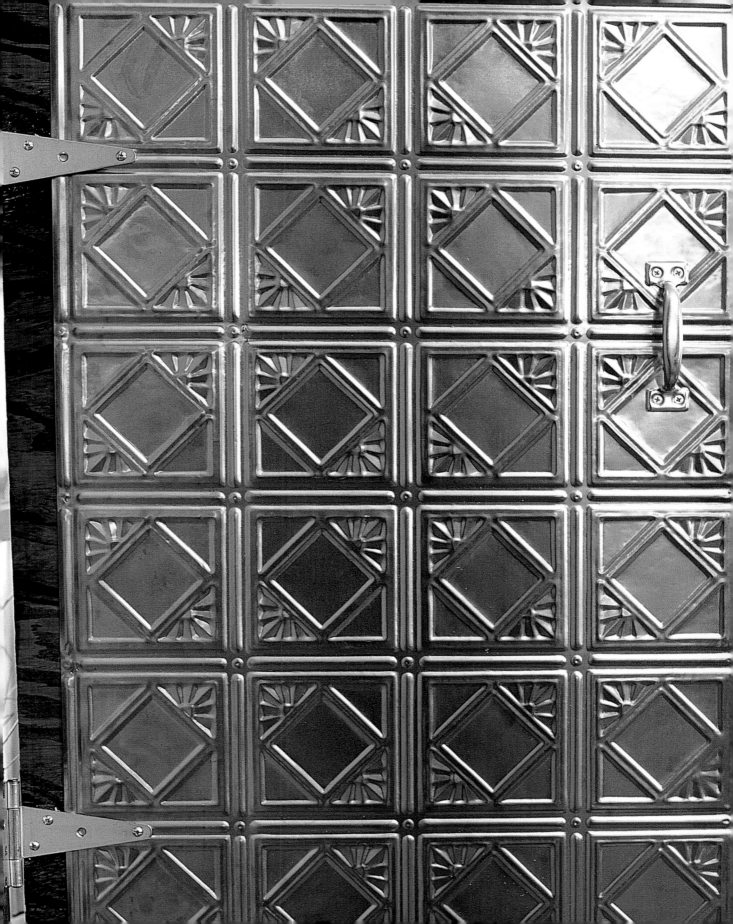

Slate and Main

Sure, you love a window box, but
have you ever seen one indoors?
Here's one that will certainly turn a
garden inside out.

Supplies

Window box (1 per window)
Precut box of slate (enough to cover
front and sides of the box)
Plastic lining
Tube of concrete glue
Nails
Strong eye hooks
Potting soil
Plant

Tools

Hammer

Rule of thumb: If you
want to open and close
the shutter, place the
box far enough below
the sill to plant and still
have room for the
shutter to move easily.

Getting Started

CREATING THE WINDOW BOX

1. Using concrete glue, attach
   slate to two ends and one side
   of the window box.
2. Screw two strong eye hooks on
   opposite ends near the top of
   box's back edge.
3. Hammer two nails halfway into
   the wall along the widow sill.
   (Their placement should match
   the distance apart of the two
   eye hooks on the box.)
4. Line the inside of the window
   box with plastic, fill with potting
   soil, and plant.
5. Hang planted box from the nails
   on the wall.

Hot Socks

What is better than wrapping yourself in flannel, wearing a warm pair of socks, and curling up with a good book? The answer—curling up next to a great pair of hanging socks!

Supplies

Wool socks
Sink strainer
Funnel
Rosco "Sculpt or Coat"
Straight pins
Light socket with cord and plug
15-watt bulb
Twine
Ceiling hook with a screw end
Murphy's Oil Soap

Tools

Paintbrush
Utility knife
Wire cutters

Getting Started

CREATING THE LAMPSHADE

1. Stretch the ankle part of the wool sock over the funnel. (The foot of the sock should be hanging off the spout of the funnel as extra fabric.)

2. Tie twine around the sock and the funnel where the funnel meets the spout.

3. Using a brush, coat the outside of the sock with "Sculpt or Coat" thinly and evenly. Let dry and harden.

4. With a utility knife, cut the sock at the base of the funnel where it meets the spout.

5. Slip the sock off the funnel. (The sock should remain in the shape of the funnel.)

6. Holding the outside of the sock (gently so as to keep its shape), paint the inside of the sock with a thin, even layer of "Sculpt or Coat."

7. Coat the funnel with a thin layer of Murphy's Oil Soap (to act as a releasing gel when you remove the sock the second time). Slip the sock back onto the funnel. (This step will keep the sock in its funnel shape until the inside is fully dry.) Let dry and harden.

8. Slip the sock off the funnel. (If it does not move readily, carefully poke a knife up in between the sock and funnel to loosen it.)

ATTACHING THE SHADE TO THE LAMP

9. With wire cutters, snip the wires of the bottom of a sink strainer in a straight slit.

10. Take an electric cord with an attached light socket, and push the plug through the slit of the strainer. Slide the strainer down the cord so it rests above the light socket.

11. Slip the top of the sock over the light socket and join the top of the sock to the strainer by poking straight pins through the strainer hole and into the sock material.

12. Screw in bulb.

13. Screw ceiling hook in desired position for lamp to hang from the ceiling.

14. Hang electric cord from the ceiling hook and plug in.

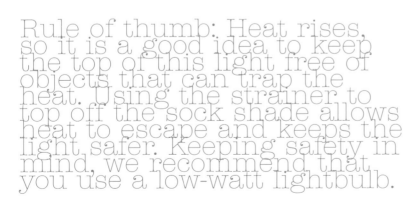

Rule of thumb: Heat rises, so it is a good idea to keep the top of this light free of objects that can trap the heat. Using the strainer to top off the sock shade allows heat to escape and keeps the light safer. Keeping safety in mind, we recommend that you use a low-watt lightbulb.

Make it chic: Copper tacks add a decorative touch to the frames.

Lowe and Behold

Remember the drive-through
banks that you used to go to with
your parents—you know, where
they gave you free lollipops? They
made me so happy. I get the same
sensation when I go to buy paint
and they give me free stir sticks.
I always take more then I could
ever use, but here I've found a way
to put them to work.

Supplies

Wood picture frame
Paint sticks
Copper tacks

Tools

Hammer

Getting Started

1. Take out backing and glass
   of picture frame.
2. Break four paint sticks to
   approximately the lengths
   of the frame sides.
3. Lay one stick over opposite
   sides of the frame. Lay one stick
   over each remaining side of the
   frame. (The sticks will overlap
   each other.)
4. Nail the sticks at all four corners
   of the frame.
5. Replace glass, insert picture,
   and reattach the back.

LIVING ROOM

Fencing Underfoot

The look of a worn wooden floor gives a room character as well as warmth—two great traits of any cabin. By turning rugged fencing into a floor you get a great look, and it's simple to do. So go ahead, be brave and turn a fence upside down.

Supplies

Sheets of stockade fence (enough sheets to cover entire floor)
Two 2 × 4 boards
Sandpaper
Stain
Polyurethane
Long wood nails

Tools

Hammer
Paintbrush
Handsaw
Tape measure
Rags

First time: Paint colors on a surface by forming a thin film. Stain colors on a surface by penetrating it.

Getting Started

MEASURING AND CUTTING THE FENCING

The floor is going to be divided into two or, in some cases, three parts. The picket fencing should be laid on its back with the pickets of one fence facing one wall and the pickets of another facing the opposite wall, with the two flat ends meeting in the middle.

1. Measure the width of the room. If the width of the room equals the width of two pieces of fencing, then step 1 ends here. If the room is wider, fill the gap by cutting pieces of fencing the length of the remaining space. (These pieces will go between the two standard lengths to act as connectors.) If the room is narrower, trim both pieces of fencing the same amount so that the two lengths together equal the width of the room.

REINFORCING THE FENCING

2. Using a hammer and nails, attach two 2 × 4s in between and parallel to the two existing crossbars on the back of the fencing. Make sure they are spaced equally. (The 2 × 4s will act as extra support bars, reinforcing the pickets.) Repeat on all pieces of fencing.

3. Sand the pickets of the fence.

PREPARING THE SURFACE OF THE FENCING

4. Stain both sides of the fencing. Repeat on all pieces and let dry.

5. Apply polyurethane to both sides of the fencing. Repeat on all pieces and let dry.

LAYING THE FLOOR

6. Lay the fencing on the floor along one wall with the pickets pointing toward the wall.

7. If it applies, lay the middle section.

8. Lay fencing down on the opposite side of the floor, remembering to face the pickets toward the wall with the flat ends facing the middle.

Tree House

You may be too old to live in a tree
house, but that doesn't mean you're
too old to live among trees.

Supplies
Natural wood branches
Cup hooks (3 pairs per branch)
Leather cord (enough to tie
branches to hooks)

Tools
Scissors

Getting Started

1. Position a branch in each
   corner and in the center of
   all four walls.
2. To secure the branch in place,
   screw three pairs of hooks into
   the wall at either side of a
   branch; screw one pair near the
   top, one pair in the center, and
   one pair near the bottom of
   each branch.
3. Tie a leather cord to one hook,
   wrap the cord over the branch,
   and tie it off around the
   second hook.

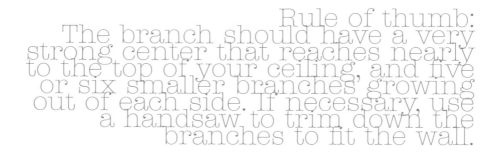

Rule of thumb:
The branch should have a very
strong center that reaches nearly
to the top of your ceiling, and five
or six smaller branches' growing
out of each side. If necessary, use
a handsaw to trim down the
branches to fit the wall.

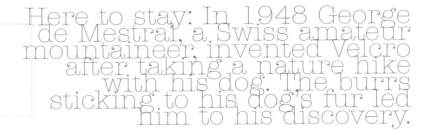

Here to stay: In 1948 George de Mestral, a Swiss amateur mountaineer, invented Velcro after taking a nature hike with his dog. The burrs sticking to his dog's fur led him to his discovery.

Bandana-Rama

This is an inexpensive way to create texture and interest on a wall. The project can easily be adapted to any look if you use different types of fabric, photographs, or swatches in simple bold colors.

Supplies

Masonite, 4 panels (length equals 4 bandanas, height equals length of 1 bandana minus 3 inches)
Bandanas (at least 16), in 4 colors
Lattice strips
Stain
Self-adhesive Velcro
Nails

Tools

Scissors
Glue gun and glue sticks
Handsaw
Hammer
Rags

Getting Started

CREATING BANDANA PANELS

1. Lay four bandanas next to each other on a Masonite panel. Alternate colors, creating a patchwork-quilt appearance. The bandanas should hang over the top, bottom, and side edges of the panel.

2. Wrap the top and bottom and two end edges of the bandanas around to the back of the panel and secure with a hot glue gun.

3. Repeat steps 1 and 2 for all four panels.

CREATING FRAMES FOR BANDANA PANELS

4. With a handsaw, cut five strips of lattice to the length of the Masonite panels. (These strips will be the horizontal edges of the quilt frame.)

5. With a handsaw, cut five strips of lattice to the total height of all Masonite panels plus the total width of all five strips of lattice. (These strips will be the vertical edges of the quilt frame.)

6. Using a rag, stain the lattice strips. Let dry.

ATTACHING THE BANDANA QUILT TO THE WALL

7. Starting from the floor, Velcro your first horizontal strips of lattice to the wall.

8. Line up one bandana panel lengthwise over the lattice strip, so that the bottom edge of the panel rests on the top edge of the strip.

9. Nail the bandanna panel to the wall.

10. Repeat steps 7–9 until all panels and strips are attached. (Remember to attach lattice strips and panels directly above each other, ending with a lattice strip at the top.)

11. Velcro a vertical lattice strip at each bandana seam.

12. Velcro one strip at either vertical edge of the quilt wall, completing the frame.

Cover Up

Adding color and texture is a great way to give new life to any sofa needing a face-lift.

Supplies

Fabric (enough to cover the seat of the sofa)
Nylon ribbon
Horn toggle buttons
Twist pins

Tools

Large upholstery needle
Scissors
Tape measure

Getting Started

MAKING THE SLIPCOVER

1. Cut enough fabric to fit the length, depth, and width of the seat portion of your sofa. You may use more than one panel of fabric.
2. Remove the back cushions of your couch and lay fabric over the seat and down to the floor. (If there is more than one panel of fabric, overlap the second panel and secure.)
3. Use twist pins to secure fabric to sofa under the seat cushions.
4. Replace pillow rests.

ATTACHING THE TOGGLE BUTTON

5. Measure approximately 1 inch in and about 5 inches up from the bottom corner of your slipcover.
6. Attach the first toggle button horizontally with an upholstery needle and nylon ribbon.

CREATING THE TOGGLE CHARM

7. Thread needle with a longer piece of ribbon. Loop through the buttonholes of a second toggle and tie both ends of thread in a knot tightly at the toggle surface, leaving about 4 inches of ribbon loose.
8. Use the loose ends to tie around the first toggle button, letting the second toggle dangle beyond edge of fabric.
9. Repeat steps 6–8 every 8 inches along the bottom edge of the slipcover.

Rocky Top

Who doesn't have some rocks collected as souvenirs over the years? Why not show off your prizes by incorporating them in a coffee table? Besides, this is another great way to bring the outdoors in.

Supplies

Coffee table (with a flat surface)
½-inch plywood (cut to fit over surface of coffee table, adding 1 inch on all sides)
Lattice (enough to border all sides of the coffee table)
Wall grout
Flat river rocks
Nails

Tools

Spatula
Hammer
Rag

Getting Started

1. Lay plywood over coffee table.
2. Cut four pieces of lattice to fit the four edges of the plywood.
3. Create a ridge around the plywood by nailing the lattice strips lengthwise to the bottom edges of the plywood. (The width of the strips should extend about ¾ inch above the surface of the plywood to create the ridgelike border.)
4. With a spatula, spread the wall grout, about ½ inch thick, flat over half the surface of the table. (The grout can dry over a short period, so it is best to work on one section at a time.)
5. Place river rocks into the wall grout, starting at the edges and moving inward. Press each rock into the wall grout firmly. Lay the stones close to one another. (Use flat rocks to create an even surface.)
6. Repeat steps 4 and 5 for the second half of the table.
7. When the grout is fairly dry, clean off any excess grout on the stone surface, using a little hot water and a rag.

Make it chic: The British artist Andy Goldsworthy uses nature in his art by participating in it as intimately as he can. He generally works with whatever he observes from the natural world—twigs, leaves, stone, snow, etc.—to make his pieces.

Run with the Bulls

This is a rustic way to hang any
type of curtain, and it continues the
creative use of branches throughout the room.

You can't go wrong:
For extra security,
squirt some wood glue
on the inside of the
horn where it will
meet the corners of
the wood peg.

Supplies

Medium horns (2 per window)
Precut square wood blocks, cut to
fit inside the circumference of the
horn's opening (2 per window)
Birch branches, the width of the
window plus 2 feet (1 per window)
Nails
Screws

Tools

Drill
Hanmer
Handsaw

Getting Started

1. Nail one wood block about
   7 inches above and about
   4 inches to the left of the
   window frame.
2. Repeat this step for the opposite
   side of the frame, this time
   7 inches above and about
   4 inches to the right of the
   frame.
3. Fit horn over wood block with
   the tip facing up.
4. Drill a screw through the top
   base of the horn and into the
   wood block underneath to
   secure it.
5. Repeat steps 3–4 for the
   second horn.
6. Lay birch in the grooves of
   the horns.

Make it chic: When cutting jeans, cut around the back pockets and incorporate them into your trim pattern. You can make many patterns with these shapes, and they are very useful to finish off corners of the curtain panel. Even the fly buttons are useful as cool detailing for decorating the top of the curtain.

Made to Fit

I know, I know, you hate throwing away your old jeans. So don't. Be a cowboy and strap them to your windows.

Supplies

Dark jeans (enough pairs to line the perimeter of curtain panel when cut in strips)
Curtain panel (1 per window)
Fabric glue

Tools

Fabric scissors

Getting Started

CUTTING THE JEANS

1. Cut jeans legs into strips 5 to 7 inches wide, leaving the natural length. (It is easy to cut jeans straight by making one initial cut about 2 inches deep into the bottom of the jeans and then ripping them lengthwise. Ripping will help create a frayed look later.)

2. Cut enough pairs of jeans to create enough strips to trim the edges of the sides and bottom of the curtain panel with room for overlapping at the ends.

ATTACHING THE JEANS TO THE CURTAINS

3. Lay pieces of jeans lengthwise along the perimeter of the curtain panel, overlapping the strips of jeans 1 inch as you travel along the edge of the curtain panel. Layer different widths of jeans over one another for that rough cowboy look. The outside edges of the jeans rectangles should extend beyond the panel edge approximately ½ inch.

4. Glue down jeans rectangles in place.

5. Cut out the back triangle pattern at the waist of the jeans, following the pattern to the outside seams of the jeans at either end.

6. Glue the triangle pattern to the center of the panel's top edge, with the tip of the triangle pointing down. If it does not reach the panel's side edge, fill in the gaps with more rectangular pieces of jeans.

Cabin Keepsake

My good friend Sarah taught me how to make my own wrap journal, and my family cottage was the first place I ever signed a guest book, which showed me that guest books are not only for signatures at gala events but for doodles and quotes that recount the activity of a home. The combination of these two memories inspired this project. Leave your cabin keepsake on your coffee table for all to browse through and, if they want, contribute to.

Supplies
Leather hide
15 large sheets of paper

Tools
Scissors
Awl

Getting Started
1. Lay leather hide on a flat surface.
2. Fold approximately fifteen sheets of paper in half and lay open over leather hide.
3. Cut leather hide around border of paper, leaving approximately 2 inches around all four sides for a book cover lip.
4. With an awl, puncture two holes through the paper along the crease and into the hide below it.
5. Cut a thin leather cord out of the excess hide.
6. Push the cord through the holes, connecting the stack of paper to the hide.
7. Tie the ends of the cord on the outside of the hide, and wrap cord around book.

Moss Art

If you only want to hint at the cabin look . . . how about a picture frame?

Supplies
Picture frame
Moss
Twigs
2 chestnuts

Tools
Small screwdriver
Hammer
Glue gun and glue sticks
Scissors

Getting Started
TWIG AND MOSS PICTURE FRAME
1. Cut pieces of moss to fit all around the edges of the frame.
2. With a hot glue gun, glue moss to frame.
3. Cut thin twigs to the length of the frame.
4. Glue twigs onto moss, overlapping them at the corners.

MOSS AND CHESTNUT PICTURE FRAME
1. Wedge a screwdriver's tip in the seam of a chestnut. With a hammer lightly break open. Repeat for second chestnut.
2. Clean out inside grooves of chestnuts with tip of screwdriver.
3. Glue one chestnut half onto each of the four corners of the frame, with the inside of the chestnut facing out.
4. Cut moss to fit frame edges in between the chestnuts.
5. With a hot glue gun, glue moss to frame.

ENCHANTED AUGUST
a seaside cottage

I grew up in a small resort town that would triple in population during the winter and summer seasons. The town served as a playground both in the winter (it was full of ski hills and chalets) and in the summer (it was full of sailboats and tennis courts). This was my hometown. And with each season that came and went I grew closer to the landscape, closer to the street lamps, and closer to the big white cottages. My hometown is Petoskey, Michigan.

Being there meant ushering out the fall and welcoming the winter, saying good-bye to the brief but sweet spring and hello to the summer. It was a life I embraced. But, just like the teacher who has a pet, I had a favorite season. Hello summer, where the days are longer, the sky is bluer, and the town is livelier.

Each summer, storeowners would migrate to my hometown from Palm Springs, Palm Beach, and any other place that was terminally warm. Theirs were not just shops but boutiques. La-di-da! They were filled with bold whites, pretty pinks, canary yellow, stripes, and plaids, patterns that were made of the best cottons, leather, and silk.

Imagine a town filled with shops loaded with bright green wide-wale corduroys decorated with ducks all over them, and streets filled with people *wearing* them! Are you getting the picture? The Hamptons, Nantucket . . . they had nothing on my little summertime village, where entire families posed for portraits wearing lime-green Lilly Pulitzer pants and dresses. There were other sights of summer streaming into our town: Julliverts restaurant would unfold its red-and-white awning and begin serving its homemade ice cream and planked whitefish. The Young Americans, a traveling musical group, would show off their long array of Broadway shows. But the best, the best part of summer was the opening of Bay View Cottages, an association of beautifully restored Victorian homes.

Oh, I could not wait.

Hurry up . . . Take the wooden shutters down! Can't you see the snow has melted into sand? The bay is full of motorboats, not ice fishing shacks. Where are your bright-colored curtains? Pull out your wicker porch furniture. Fill your pots with red geraniums. The birds have arrived and so my town must be full of tourists.

I could not wait for the fresh breeze the tourists seemed to bring with them. I rarely got to stand in their white fortresses, but when I did I was never disappointed by their charm.

The summer blues and greens in this chapter try to re-create the look of Petoskey's Bay View Cottages. They had rooms filled with homages to the months of June, July, and August. To me, these rooms would make anyone feel at home anytime of the year.

BEDROOM

Deep Blue Sea

There are so many wonderful things about the sea, and one of my favorite tricks is to stare straight ahead into vast ocean, then quickly turn to the right, then the left, and back again. With every turn, I spot a new hue of the color.

Supplies

6 pieces of luan
3 shades of blue paint
Sandpaper
Industrial strength Velcro

Tools

Paint roller handle
3 paint rollers
Paint rolling pan
3 rolling pan inserts

Getting Started

1. At your lumberyard, cut equal size squares of luan to cover your entire floor.
2. Sand surface and edges of squares.
3. Divide your squares up evenly into three groups and paint each group one color, using three colors in total. Let dry.
4. Lay down the squares on your floor. Mix up the squares so no two squares of the same color lie next to each other.
5. Velcro all the corners of the squares to the floor.

Grab that look: For a shiny look, use three shades of enamel paint.

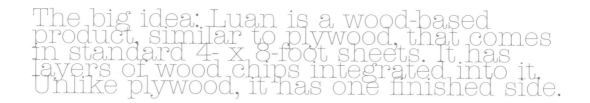

The big idea: Luan is a wood-based product, similar to plywood, that comes in standard 4- x 8-foot sheets. It has layers of wood chips integrated into it. Unlike plywood, it has one finished side.

Gathering Shells

When I once asked someone in my workshop to do research and find out why it is that shells carry the sound of the ocean, one of my faithful employees held a cup to my ear to illustrate that it too carries the sound of the ocean. As I sank into my chair, another employee shouted, "Oh, yeah, and Santa Claus is also real." All right, shells are not magic, but they still look great as a decoration in any room by the sea, or not by the sea.

Supplies

1- × 6-inch pine planks (enough to create a baseboard and a ceiling board on all walls)
3 shades of blue paint
Thick rope
Seashells and starfish
Nails

Tools

Glue gun and glue sticks
Hammer
Tape measure
Paintbrushes

Getting Started

1. Paint wall light blue. Let dry.
2. Measure and cut enough planks to run along the entire length of all four walls twice, thus creating a set of planks for the ceiling board and another set for the baseboard.
3. Paint baseboard set the second shade of blue. Let dry.
4. Paint ceiling board set the third shade of blue. Let dry.
5. Nail one plank to the wall along the bottom edge on the floor, creating a baseboard.
6. Cut one length of heavyweight rope. Hot-glue the rope to the top edge of the baseboard.
7. Repeat steps 5 and 6 for the entire room.
8. Nail the second plank about 1 foot down from the ceiling, parallel to the baseboard, creating the ceiling board.
9. Cut two lengths of heavyweight rope, and hot-glue one to the top edge of the ceiling board and one to the bottom edge.
10. Repeat steps 8 and 9 for the entire room.
11. Hot-glue seashells and starfish to the baseboard in various places, creating a natural, random pattern.

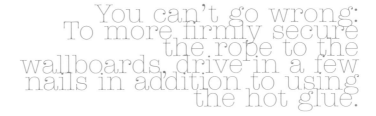

You can't go wrong: To more firmly secure the rope to the wallboards, drive in a few nails in addition to using the hot glue.

Dreamcatcher

When I was a little girl, I always thought canopy beds were for grown-ups—they seemed so luxurious and romantic. So to add a touch of sophistication to the casual look of a summer house, we have created a rugged but charming canopy.

Supplies

13 thick bamboo shoots (each approximately 8 feet long)
16 L brackets
Screws
Thick leather ribbon
Patio cushions

Tools

Screwdriver
Handsaw
Scissors
Tape measure

Getting Started

CREATING THE HEAD OF THE CANOPY

1. Lay two uncut bamboo shoots on the floor. (These shoots will act as bedposts.)
2. Cut three bamboo shoots the width of the bed.
3. Lay one bamboo shoot between the bamboo bedposts 2 inches down from the top (this will be the first of three horizontal crossbars parallel to each other that will hold the headboard posts together). Attach the crossbar to the posts using screws and two L brackets.
4. Measure from the bottom of the bedposts to where the top of the mattress will come. With two more L brackets and screws, attach the second crossbar.
5. Place a third crossbar 40 inches above the crossbar placed in step 4. With two more L brackets and screws, attach the crossbar.

CREATING THE BASEBOARD OF THE CANOPY

6. Repeat steps 1–4 for the foot of the bed.

CREATING THE SIDES OF THE CANOPY

7. Cut four bamboo shoots the length of the bed to create two bars for each side.
8. Lay the headboard on the floor.
9. Measure and mark on both bedposts the height of the bottom of the mattress.
10. Where marked, use screws and L brackets to attach the side bars onto each of the bedposts perpendicularly.
11. Connect second set of side bars 2 inches down from the top of each bedpost, perpendicular to the headboard. (These side bars should be the same height as the top crossbars on the headboard.)
12. Turn the structure upright and place at the head of the bed, with the side bars running parallel to the length of the mattress.
13. Using L brackets and screws, attach the baseboard to the four side bars.

CREATING THE FINISHING TOUCHES

14. Wrap and tie leather ribbon around all the joints to hide the L brackets.
15. Hang two patio cushions from the middle headboard crossbar.

Sheer Delight

If you don't have a cool ocean breeze at your disposal, sheers hung in abundance are a great way to feel as if you are at the seaside. The way they move, the way they hang, and the way they fall echo the movements of the wind.

Supplies
Gauze fabric
Stitch Witchery

Tools
Pinking shears
Tape measure

Getting Started

1. Measure the length from the top of your bed frame to the floor, and add on an extra 1½ feet (6 inches for the top ties and 1 foot for a puddle at the bottom).
2. Cut six panels to this length. Using the Stitch Witchery, create a 1-inch hem at the bottom of each panel.
3. With shears, cut four evenly spaced slits 6 inches deep along the top of your panel.
4. Cut down the center of each slit, forming two sides of a tie.
5. Tie the panels onto the two bottom corners of the bamboo canopy. Let the excess fabric in between the tabs fall naturally as a rustic detail.

Make it chic:
If you don't
want to use a
comforter
cover, simply
decorate your
pillowcases.

Dragonfly Dreams

One thing to keep in mind when
you are decorating a summer
room is to include the motifs of
mother nature.

Supplies
Comforter cover
Fabric paint
Thin cardboard
Paper plate
Newsprint

Tools
Stencil brush
Scissors
Pencil

Getting Started
1. Cut cardboard into a 7-inch
   square.
2. Fold cardboard in half.
3. Draw half of a bug shape along
   the crease.
4. Cut the folded cardboard along
   the outline so that when it is
   unfolded a complete bug shape
   will emerge.
5. Pour some fabric paint onto a
   paper plate.

6. Lay comforter cover flat on a
   table. Put some newsprint inside
   the comforter where you will be
   stenciling, to prevent the paint
   from bleeding to the next layer.
7. Position your stencil on one
   corner of your comforter.
8. Paint inside stencil using the
   stencil brush.
9. Carefully move the stencil to
   the next location and repeat
   painting all along the borders
   of the cover.

Linen Layer

What is better than lying on the
grass and looking up at the stars?
When you can't camp out, you can
at least rest your mattress on a skirt
reminiscent of a big open field.

Supplies
Sea grass (2 handfuls)
Bed skirt
White paint
Newsprint
Heavy-duty paper plate

Tools
Scissors

Getting Started
1. Lay one side of the bed skirt
   lengthwise on a table.
2. Cut a bundle of sea grass so the
   tallest grass is a bit shorter than
   the height of the bed skirt.
3. Fill a heavy-duty paper plate
   halfway with white paint.
4. Place a bundle of grass on
   some newsprint. Paint the grass
   with white paint.
5. Press the painted grass onto the
   bed skirt (so the grass appears
   to be growing from the bottom
   of the skirt to the top). Lay a fresh
   piece of newsprint over the
   grass and carefully press down,
   forcing the white paint onto the
   bed skirt. Try not to move the
   grass underneath, as you want
   the impression to stay as true to
   the grass stems as possible.
6. Carefully lift up the grass from
   the skirt.
7. Repeat the impressions side by
   side until the whole bed skirt is
   covered.

Beach Treasures

Nature supplies design in just
about every leaf, blade of grass,
and cloud. One of my favorite ways
nature shows off is in the creases,
crinkles, and curves of driftwood.
Simply by using driftwood, you
have something well crafted.

Keep it simple:
If some pieces of
driftwood are too
long or do not fit at
particular corners,
cut the branches
with a handsaw and
then attach them.

Supplies

Wood shelving unit

Eye hooks

20-gauge wire

Driftwood branches

White spray paint

Tools

Wire cutters

Getting Started

1. Approximately every 10 inches,
   screw in eye hooks around the
   perimeter of the frame and the
   shelves of the unit.

2. Cut your wire into 10-inch-
   long pieces.

3. Choose driftwood pieces by
   seeing which ones look best
   parallel to the frame.

4. Using the wire, attach the
   driftwood to the eye hooks on
   the unit. (Allow any twisted
   driftwood to break and overlap
   with the frame.)

5. When the entire shelf unit
   is covered to your satisfaction,
   spray-paint the whole unit
   white, or another color of
   your choice.

Paddle to the Sea

A great way to include something nautical in a room is to discover its usefulness. A paddle is the perfect tool both on the water and off.

Supplies

Paddles (1 per window)
White nylon rope
Loosely woven linen fabric
Coat hooks with 2 prongs (2 per window)
Starfish
Fabric glue

Tools

Scissors
Screwdriver
Screws
Tape measure

Getting Started

CREATING THE CURTAIN PANEL

1. Screw two coat hooks above the top two corners of the window frame.
2. Measure the length from the top of the coat hooks to the floor, and add on 1½ feet (6 inches for the hems and 1 foot for a puddle at the bottom).
3. Cut a panel of fabric to this measurement, leaving the width of the fabric as is. (Cut as many panels as needed to cover the width of the window.)
4. Hem the top and the bottom of the panel by folding the fabric over 3 inches. Use fabric glue to secure.
5. Using the tips of the scissors, poke a hole approximately every 10 inches and 2 inches down from the top of the panel.
6. Gently pull out the loose threads around the holes with your hand to give the panel a frayed, rustic look.
7. Cut 1 foot of white nylon rope for each hole and thread through.
8. Tie each rope around the paddle and knot it together.
9. Place paddle on top prong of the coat hooks.

STARFISH ORNAMENTS

10. Cut a piece of rope to ⅓ the length of the curtain panel.
11. Wrap and tie starfish at random places on the rope.
12. Tie the rope in a loop at one end. Hang loop on the lower prong of the coat hook.
13. Repeat steps 10–12 for the opposite side of the panel.

Knotical

Creating lamps out of unusual
pieces has become much easier
with all the tools and kits available
these days. So it is possible to charm
a nautical rope into a lamp—perfect
for any bedside table.

Supplies

Thick nautical rope
(approximately 4 feet)
10-gauge steel wire
(approximately 4 feet)
Small, plain lampshade
2 colors of papyrus paper
(1 sheet each)
4-inch-long brass tubing
(approximately the same diameter
as the rope)
Thin packing twine
Electric cord with end plug
Rubber socket
(that fits the brass tube)
Lightbulb
Spray adhesive

Tools

Scissors
Metal ruler
Tape measure
Wire strippers

Getting Started

MAKING THE LAMP BASE

1. Cut 3 feet of the nautical rope.
2. Cut 3 feet of 10-gauge steel wire.
3. Thread wire through inside
   of rope.

4. Tie the rope into a large knot.
   Pull the top end of the rope up
   so that it extends approximately
   8 inches out of the knot. (This is
   the neck where the lightbulb
   will be attached.)
5. Create a 2-inch-wide band
   around the other end of the
   rope by wrapping and tying
   with twine.

MAKING THE LAMPSHADE

6. Measure and mark the papyrus
   into 3-inch-wide strips that are
   long enough to cover the height
   of your shade plus 1 inch.
   (Create enough strips to go all
   the way around the shade.)
7. Fold, press, and then unfold
   along the lines marked in step 6.
   Using a ruler as a straightedge,
   rip along the fold to separate
   the strips. (Leave the edges
   rough and frayed to add to the
   sea-worn look.)
8. With spray adhesive, attach
   strips of papyrus to the
   lampshade, alternating colors
   and overlapping the strips.

LIGHTING

9. Attach electric cord to rubber
   socket by stripping the cord's
   two copper conductors with
   wire strippers.
10. Wind each of the two conductors
    around one of the screws on the
    socket. Tighten screws over
    copper wires.
11. Fit the bottom of the socket
    into the brass tube, with the
    electric cord hanging out the
    opposite side.
12. Place the brass tube and socket
    over the end of the rope.
13. Wrap and tuck the electric cord
    in and around the rope to
    conceal it. Feed the plug end
    of the cord through the heart of
    the knot so that it hangs down
    and can easily fall off the side
    of a table.
14. Screw a bulb into the socket and
    place the lampshade on top.

You can't go wrong: If the socket is too small for the brass tubing, wrap electric tape around the socket until the brass tube holds it well.

Checkerboard Squares

With this board, not only is checkers
a great way to pass a rainy day;
it's a great way to use all the buckets
of seashells and starfish you
are forever gathering.

Supplies

4 slate squares
Paint
Seashells
Starfish
Luan square
(cut to total size of all 4 squares)

Tools

Paintbrush
Masking tape
Concrete glue

Getting Started

1. Using concrete glue, attach
   four squares of slate to Luan.
2. Divide slate into eight equal
   squares per row vertically and
   horizontally.
3. Starting with the first row, tape
   off sides of every other square.
4. Paint inside taped-off squares.
   Let dry. Remove tape.
5. Repeat steps 2 and 3 on every
   row, until checkerboard is
   complete.
6. Place starfish on one side of the
   checkerboard and seashells on
   the other.

Sandtastic

This is a perfect sand castle. Why?
Because it won't drift away with the
tide, despite what Jimi Hendrix
sings: "So castles made of sand fall
in the sea . . . eventually."

Supplies

Self-hardening clay
White glue
Cup
Sand
Newspaper

Tools

Paintbrush

Make it chic: To imitate the drip castles you make by the sea, roll small balls of clay and push them together to create a base. Add more balls, forming a straight tower until you come to the tip.

Getting Started

1. Build a castle out of your molding
   clay. Place on newspaper.
   Let dry.
2. Pour some white glue into a
   cup and paint the surface of the
   castle with white glue.
3. Pour sand over the castle,
   covering all the glue. Let dry.

LIVING ROOM

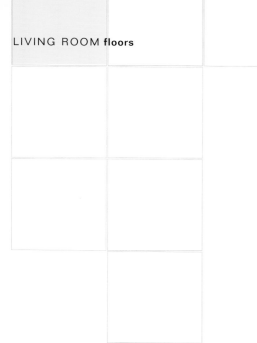

Tiptoe Through the Tulips

You know the song "Everything Old Is New Again"? It was written as a love song to this project. Okay, maybe not, but you can bring life to an old rug simply by adding a new patch of fabric.

Supplies
Oval braided rug
Chintz fabric
Thin ribbon (in a color complementary to the fabric)

Tools
Upholstery needle
Pinking shears
Fabric scissors

Getting Started

1. Cut fabric to size for rug. (This doesn't have to be precise, because the fabric will be trimmed further later.)
2. Place fabric on top of rug.
3. Using upholstery needle threaded with ribbon, attach fabric to the rug four rows in from the outside edge. (Simply pull the needle and thread through one side and out and through the other, and tie the two ends together, creating a knot on the top of the fabric.)
4. Repeat threading and knotting every 4 inches around the perimeter of rug.
5. Count from edge of rug eight rows in from the first set of ribbons and create a second inner circle of securing knots.
6. To finish, trim fabric with pinking sheers 1 inch from the outer ribbon circle.

You can't go wrong: You can change the fabric easily with this method.

Shutterbug

If you can't afford art, create your
own. And you don't have to be
an artist to be crafty: Just use
something that is common and
repeat it over a large space.

Supplies
Plastic shutters
Screws
Plastic buttons
Primer
Paint

Tools
Screwdriver
Paintbrush
Glue gun and glue sticks

You can't go wrong:
Plastic shutters are
lightweight, making
installation easy.

Getting Started
1. Prime and paint shutters.
2. Starting at the bottom corner of
   the shutter, attach a screw
   1 inch in from each corner
   through the shutter to the wall.
3. Continue placing shutters in
   different directions—some
   vertically, others horizontally—
   in a seemingly haphazard
   pattern. You can leave spaces
   between shutters so that all the
   shutters fit on the wall without
   needing to be cut.
4. Once all the shutters are in place,
   cover each screw by hot-gluing a
   plastic button over it.

Tailored Trellis

Mary, Mary, quite contrary, where does your garden grow? On the back of my sofa.

Supplies
4 large wood finials
(with screw in bottom)
Ribbon, 4 inches wide
Trellis

Tools
Fabric scissors
Handsaw

Getting Started
1. Cut one piece of trellis the height and length of the sofa.
2. Cut two pieces of trellis the height and length of the sides of the sofa.
3. Screw two finials onto the top front and back ends of each arm.
4. String ribbon through back trellis and tie around each finial.
5. Trim ribbon ends at a 45-degree angle.
6. Repeat steps 4 and 5 for the three remaining arm trellises.

Totally Towels

Reupholstering can cost an arm and a leg; besides, I happen to love collecting and displaying vintage dish towels. They are mini works of art and make any room feel homey.

Supplies
Safety pins
Dish towels
Thread

Tools
Needle

Getting Started
1. With a needle and thread, connect the dish towels, end to end, to create a runner that extends from the bottom of the back of the chair, over the top, down under the seat cushion, and out, touching the floor.
2. Place runner on chair and secure with safety pins on the bottom of the back of the chair.
3. With a needle and thread, connect some dish towels end to end to create a runner that extends from the bottom of the side arm, over the arm, under the seat cushion, and over and around the opposite side arm.
4. Fold the new runner in half lengthwise and place on chair.
5. With a needle and thread, connect the remaining dish towels, end to end, creating a runner the length from the end of the arm, around the back of the chair, to the end of the opposite arm.
6. Fold this runner in half lengthwise and connect to the chair with safety pins (connect the safety pins under the fold to conceal).

Yes, you can: Using safety pins instead of sewing allows you to remove towels and launder easily.

Don't Fence Me In

I am constantly looking for great ways to display collections. But just like a grumpy store clerk, I want people to look but not touch. By creating a peekaboo cover for this bookshelf, I can remain calm as I let my visitors enjoy my hobby.

Supplies
1 bookcase
1 roll of short picket fence
(slats approximately the width
of the bookcase)
2 hinges
1 metal handle
Screws

Tools
Screwdriver
Wire cutters

Getting Started
1. Attach a hinge to the top of each side of the bookcase.
2. Screw the other side of the hinge to the end slat of the picket fence.
3. Unroll picket fence.
4. With wire cutters, trim the picket fence where it meets the floor.
5. Screw handle onto a slat, approximately four slats from the floor.

Rows of Hose

What better way to bring the
outdoors in than to rob the garden
of its hose?

Supplies
4 lawn garden hoses
Rope
Glass tabletop
Epoxy

Tools
Utility knife

Getting Started

1. Keep the hoses in their original
   strapping.
2. With a utility knife, cut four
   pieces of rope long enough to
   wrap twice around the width of
   the hose.
3. Wrap and tie off rope in four
   evenly spaced places around
   the circumference of the hose.
   (Keep rope knots on the inside
   of the hose stack so that they
   will not show.)
4. Once rope is secured on all four
   hoses, cut off plastic stripping.
5. Make two stacks of two hoses.
   Place stacks about 1 foot apart.
6. Place glass on top of hoses and
   secure with epoxy.

Make it chic:
A glass-cutting store will cut a piece of
glass to any specifications. Many stores
will also bevel the edges for you. Beveling
is the grinding of the glass at an angle
along its edge that gives the glass a sort
of prismatic effect and an overall
brighter, more interesting, and more
finished look.

Rule of thumb: The spray adhesive will not harm windows. Just use a delabeler fluid once you decide to remove the cellophane.

Seeing Green

It is always a struggle to let the sun shine in and, at the same time, protect your privacy. But here's a great way to see the world through different colors while showing the world only one color.

Supplies

Colored cellophane
Flat paint stick (to smooth out cellophane)
Spray adhesive

Tools

Rotary cutter
Metal ruler
Cutting mat

Getting Started

1. On a cutting mat, measure with a metal ruler 4- × 5-inch squares. (Size of squares may vary, depending on the proportions of your window.) Cut cellophane using a rotary cutter.
2. Using spray adhesive, spray one side of a square.
3. Starting from the top, position square on the window.
4. Using the edge of a paint stick, flatten the cellophane onto the window.
5. Repeat steps 2–4 for each remaining square, working down and overlapping each square slightly to create a patchwork design.

Sheer Happiness

When I was a little girl, I shared a
room with my sister Marlee. We had
frilly, lacy, ruffled curtains. Every
night as I fell asleep, depending on
my mood, I would see monsters or
angels living in the folds. They made
for quite colorful dreams. Nowadays
my life is full of true drama, so I
prefer a simply hung sheer.

Supplies
Natural rope
Sheer fabric
2 screws

Tools
Fabric scissors
Screwdriver
Needle and thread
Utility knife
Tape measure

Getting Started
1. Cut fabric the length of the
   window height plus 7 inches for
   seam allowance. Leave the
   width of the fabric as is. (Cut as
   many panels as needed to
   cover the width of the window.)
2. Fold over top of fabric 6 inches,
   creating a wide pocket for rope
   to pass through. Sew pocket.
3. To make a hem, fold over 1 inch
   along the bottom. Sew seam in
   place.
4. With screwdriver, drive a screw
   into each top window corner.
5. String rope through curtain
   pockets, leaving 1 foot of rope
   at either end.
6. Tie off rope to screws in window,
   and leave enough rope to fall to
   the ground.
7. Trim rope with utility knife.

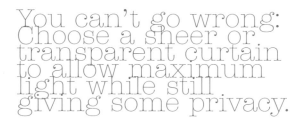

You can't go wrong:
Choose a sheer or
transparent curtain
to allow maximum
light while still
giving some privacy.

You can't go wrong: While plastic or metal rakes could work, all-wood rakes have a cleaner, rustic look.

Rake It In

Standing lamps can provide focus in a room in addition to giving light. So, when choosing one, you want to make sure it echoes the room's design motif.

Supplies

3 wood rakes
Wire, medium gauge
Light socket
Light cord, fabric-wrapped
Light plug
Lightbulb
Light brace
3-inch threaded rod for lighting
Rope

Tools

Wire strippers
Wire cutters
Electric drill and drill bit
Screwdriver
Pencil

Getting Started

1. Stand three rakes together to create a tripod.
2. Tie the rakes together with wire where the fan parts meet, one on the top and one in the middle, at all three joints. Snip any excess wire for a clean look. Cover with rope.
3. To create the light assembly, split the light cord's wires by cutting the fabric about 2 inches.
4. Strip the plastic from the wire with wire strippers to about 2 inches down on the wire.
5. With a screwdriver, attach each end of wire to each tiny screw in the socket.
6. Threading the light cord through the threaded rod piece, screw threaded rod into socket base.
7. Thread light brace onto threaded rod and socket assembly.
8. Place light assembly in rake unit.
9. Make a mark with a pencil where the light brace sits tightly inside the rakes.
10. Remove assembly and drill two holes, 1 inch apart from where you made your pencil mark.
11. Cut two pieces of wire and place one on both sides of the light brace.
12. Place light unit back in rake tripod.
13. Thread wires through drilled holes and tie off on both sides.
14. Run fabric cord down through rake handles.
15. Secure with wire rake handles and fabric cord where rake handle meets the fan of the rake.
16. Attach plug to fabric cord.
17. Place lightbulb in socket.

Dancing Lanterns

Nothing reminds me of summer more than the sun setting and a campfire roaring. When you are creating lighting for a summer look, it's great to try and re-create this flickering magic.

Supplies

Small roof hood
Small metal steamer
(1 per roof hood)
Tall drinking glasses
(1 per roof hood)
Sand
Votive candle (1 per roof hood)
Wire
Rope, medium thickness
Twine
Large eye hook (1 per roof hood)
Large cup hook (1 per roof hood)

Tools

Wire cutters
Drill
Utility knife
Tape measure

Getting Started

CREATING THE LANTERN

1. With an electric drill, drill a hole in the top of the roof hood slightly smaller than the eye hook.
2. Screw eye hook into roof hood top.
3. Measure the length of the roof hood and cut a piece of wire twice this length.
4. Tie the wire around the side arm of the roof hood, pull down through the inside of the roof hood, and thread through a hole on the bottom of the steamer; then pull up through a hole on the opposite side of the steamer. Continue pulling it up the inside of the opposite side of the roof hood and wrap around the opposite arm. Secure and tie off.
5. For more support, repeat steps 3 and 4 to include the third arm on the roof hood.

MAKING THE GLASS VOTIVE CANDLE

6. Fill drinking glasses with sand and place candle on sand.
7. Loosen one wire in order to place the votive candle on the steamer.
8. Place glass inside steamer and roof hood. (Remember to leave enough room for oxygen between drinking glass and roof hood, so that the candle will remain lit.)
9. Light the candle and resecure the wire.

HANGING THE LANTERN

10. Thread twine through eye hook and create a small loop. Bring the two ends of the twine together and tie a knot.
11. Measure from ceiling to desired height of hanging lantern.
12. Cut rope at double this measurement and add 10 inches.
13. Thread rope through the twine. Bring the two rope ends together and tie a knot.
14. Screw large cup hook to ceiling.
15. Hang rope from cup hook.

The big idea: The longest rope ever made was for a tug-of-war. It measured 564 feet 4 inches long and had a diameter of 5 feet ½ inch. The longest time spent on a tightrope was 205 days.

Sailor's Knot

Every time I go to a thrift store,
swap meet, or garage sale, I fall
in love—with fabric swatches.
I usually come home with all these
squares and panels, never having
any idea what to do with them. It's
not as though I were in the mood to
sew or to create a masterpiece;
I just wanted to have the fabric
now. This project is perfect for
instant gratification.

Supplies
Pillow forms
Medium rope
Chintz fabric

Tools
Utility knife
Pinking shears

Getting Started

1. As if you were creating a
   wrapper for a piece of hard
   candy, use pinking shears to cut
   a square of fabric large enough
   to wrap around the pillow, with
   approximately 1 foot extra to
   gather on each side.
2. Place pillow in the center of the
   fabric. Pull both ends over the
   top of the pillow.
3. Gather up the fabric on the
   sides of the pillow and secure
   by wrapping with a rope and
   tying it in a knot. With a utility
   knife, trim the ends of the rope.

The big idea:
Pinking shears
leave a raw but
decorative edge
that is less
likely to fray.

THROUGH THE LOOKING GLASS
a child's playroom

One night during the fall of 2000, the phone rang. It was my five-year-old nephew Paul, calling to tell me, with some concern, that the state of "Fornia" (better known as California) did not have enough lights. At the time, the state of California was issuing a mandatory lights out because of worsening power shortages. Not to worry. He had accumulated a collection of flashlights. Next subject: When was I coming? He advised me to leave New York at once so I could get to his house by nightfall, just in time for "Fornia's" mandatory lights-out.

What an invitation! How could his favorite aunt—a title I drilled into his little head at an early age—not come? And what could I bring to the sleepover that could compete with a government-supplied blackout? So I did it. I said, "Yes, Paul, and I'll bring the tent."

Eureka! Plans set, we hung up the phone after professing our mutual love and excitement.

The next day came and went. The next week came and went. Before I knew it, it had almost been a full month and I still had not gone to visit my precious little nephew. The guilt began to haunt me. Aunting 101: Don't make promises you cannot keep. I found comfort in knowing that Christmas was fast approaching, and I knew I could be "Fornia" bound.

Soon I was on a plane making my way across the country. Gifts? Yes. Toothbrush? Yes. Ski sweaters? Yes. Tent? No. No! How could I forget? Paul often told me that Jedi Knights never forget a promise. When my parents met me at the gate, one of the first things they mentioned was how Paul had been anxiously awaiting my arrival for days . . . and something about a tent. I explained to them,

"Well, you see...the tent. I sort of forgot the tent." My parents went white. They looked ashen, confused. So I repeated that I forgot the tent. My parents looked crushed. "You don't have the tent?" they asked. "What part of 'I forgot the tent' don't you understand?" I replied. "Are you sure he said tent?" I asked, knowing full well that the answer was yes. We walked on in silence.

When we arrived at Paul's house, with open arms and a long squeal, "Aunt Katie," he jumped into my arms. Wow! He looked in my pockets, in my bags. He smiled and asked, "Where are you hiding the tent?"

"Bing," I called out in a desperate plea to my younger brother. "I thought this vacation would be a good time for you and me to teach young scout Paul how to pitch a tent." (Bing was the only person little Paul truly believed was a Jedi Knight, and including him would certainly buy me some time.) Bing looked up only to make some sort of grumbling noise and resumed his channel surfing. I rebounded without my brother: "You see, we must wait until the time is right, and then all will be revealed to you, young, talented Jedi in training." It worked. Paul held his breath with excitement and ran off to his next project. I had a project of my own, and I called out, "Dad, give me the car keys. I need to go on a mission to find a tent."

Nightfall came, and I was prepared. Paul, his younger sister Charlie, baby Jack, and I all huddled around my brother, or should I say, the Jedi Knight, who was speaking in hushed tones about the importance of being able to assemble a tent in the dark. "A warrior never knows where or when he might land," Bing explained. "This is why I have practiced pitching my tent blindfolded." We all gasped with admiration as the bright blue bundle of shelter came together, nestled nicely next to Paul's bed. "Hey, Bing, could you zip us in?" we screamed, trying to catch him before he left the room. Wait! Paul popped on the flashlight, "Aunt Katie, this is the best tent I ever had." "Little Paul," I said, "this is the only tent you ever had." We both giggled and drifted off to sleep. The vacation, and my reputation, had been saved.

That night, my nephew Paul taught me that making a home for kids means keeping it fun.

BEDROOM

Home Turf

This project takes me back to my childhood swimming lessons at Nub's Nob, the only pool in town. The patio was covered in textured cement, and the prickly feeling under my feet would send me into fits of laughter. I believe Astro Turf, or any other textured floor covering, will give your toddler the same delight.

Supplies
Green Astro Turf
Blue Astro Turf
Carpet glue

Tools
Scissors
Tape measure

Getting Started
1. Pick which color rug you'd like to have as the base.
2. Measure this piece to the desired size for your room, keeping in mind that you want 5 extra inches on all four sides to create a hem. Cut.
3. Measure the piece that will be placed on top of the first rug 12 inches smaller than the base.
4. Using carpet glue, make a hem around the entire perimeter of the rug 5 inches wide. Repeat this step on second rug.
5. Place the smaller piece on top in the center of the larger piece.

6. Using carpet glue, secure the smaller piece in place. (It should look as if the larger piece is framing the smaller piece, acting as a border.)
7. Let glue dry thoroughly.

The Hole Story

A great way to add character as well as storage space to a room is to cover the entire wall space with Peg-Board. If you don't want to cover the room, just pick one wall. Think of it as a toolshed for juniors.

Supplies
4- × 8-feet sheets of white Peg-Board
Wood screws
2 × 4 plywood
Peg-Board hooks

Keep it simple: Peg-Board comes in white, so no painting is needed, but you can paint it if you'd like to add color to the room.

Tools
Power drill

Getting Started
1. For each piece of Peg-Board, attach two pieces of plywood to the wall, parallel to each other. Mark your wall every 4 feet and use the marks as your guide to attach your plywood strips. (The reason for the plywood is to create enough distance from the wall so that you can insert your Peg-Board hooks; it will also help prevent wall damage.)
2. Using a power drill and screws, drill screws into several holes around the outside edge of the Peg-Board, securing the Peg-Board to the plywood.
3. Repeat steps 1 and 2 until you have covered the desired areas in your room.
4. Insert Peg-Board hooks wherever they're needed.

Rigged for Romping

We pitched a tent because my nephew Paul is an aspiring Jedi Knight. If you have a budding actress in your family this could easily become her stage curtain, with slight alterations, or for a young astronaut it could be his own little space odyssey.

PART 1: MAKING THE TENT FRAME

Supplies

4 pieces of PVC pipe 1 inch in diameter (the pieces should be proportionally smaller than the bed to create a rectangle)
4 PVC pipe connectors
Cotton clothesline
2 pulleys with plastic wheels
Peg-Board
Peg-Board hooks or screw hooks

Tools

Scissors
Handsaw
Tape measure

Getting Started

CONSTRUCTING THE TENT FRAME

1. On the floor, form a rectangle with the four pieces of PVC pipe and connect them with the PVC connectors.

2. Run one piece of clothesline 2 feet long through a pulley wheel.

3. Secure one pulley to the PVC frame by tying one end of the clothesline to one corner of the frame, the other end to opposite corner.

4. Repeat steps 2 and 3 for the second pulley. (Make sure you keep the frame an equal distance from the pulley on both sides so that your tent height will be even.)

ATTACHING THE FRAME TO THE CEILING

5. Attach a Peg-Board hook to the top of the Peg-Board on each of the opposing walls. They should be the same distance between the two pulleys. If you didn't attach the Peg-Board wall detailed on page 215, attach two screw hooks to the wall.

6. Measure two pieces of clothesline, each about 2 feet longer than the width of the room. (The extra length is what you will use to adjust the tent up and down). Cut.

7. Take the end of one piece of clothesline and secure it around the hook in the wall. Do the same with the second piece of clothesline and the other hook in the same wall.

8. String each piece of clothesline through the pulleys that are attached to the PVC frame.

9. Stretch the clotheslines to the opposite side of the room and secure their ends onto the hooks that have been placed in the Peg-Board on that side of the wall. (You can adjust the height at this time; the PVC frame should hang evenly, approximately 5 feet above the mattress.)

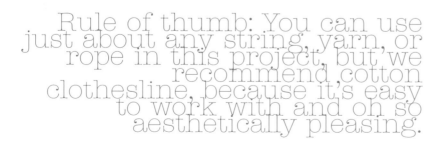

Rule of thumb: You can use just about any string, yarn, or rope in this project, but we recommend cotton clothesline, because it's easy to work with and oh so aesthetically pleasing.

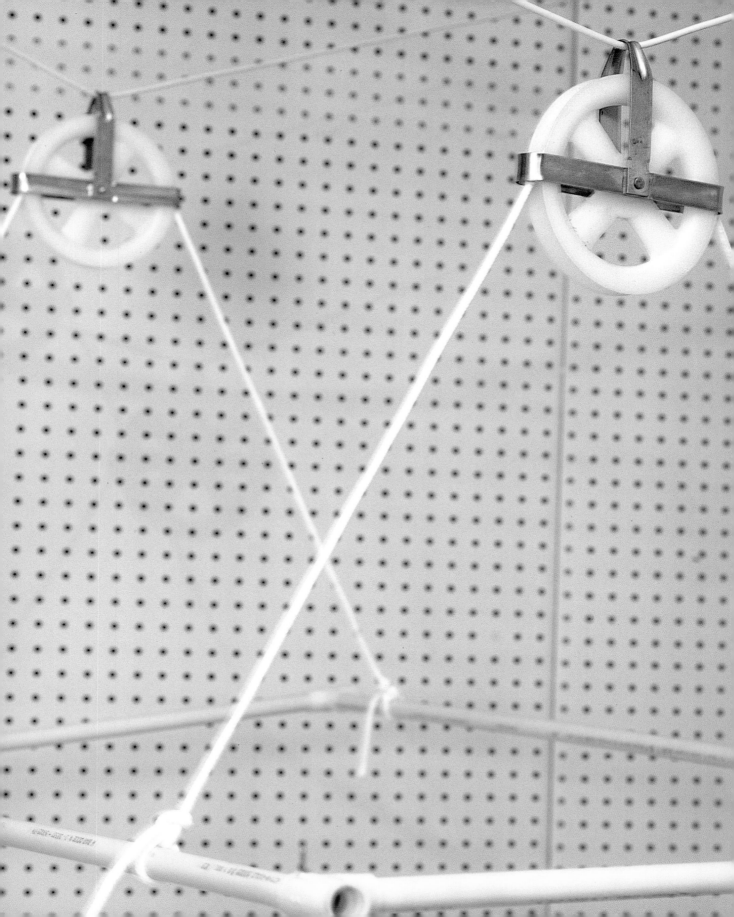

We're not done yet. What's a tent frame without a tent?

PART 2: MAKING THE TENT

Supplies

Cotton clothesline
Clothespins
Fabric for 8 curtain panels
Contrasting fabric for curtain ring

Tools

Pinking shears
Magic marker
Tape measure

Getting Started

CREATING THE PANELS

1. Measure the space between the PVC frame that you just made and the floor.
2. Measure eight panels of fabric to this measurement, adding a few extra inches in order to leave a nice puddle of fabric on the floor. Also add 1 foot more of fabric to connect it to the PVC frame.
3. Cut.

4. Attach two panels to each end of all four sides of the PVC frame, by draping 1 foot of each panel around the top of the pipe. Secure each in place by gathering all the fabric together tightly under the pipe and tying it off with a piece of 4-inch clothesline.
5. Continue until all eight panels are attached.

RING AROUND THE TENT

6. Measure the distance around the PVC frame, allowing a few extra inches for error and overlap.
7. Lay out your contrasting fabric and cut it to half of the length of your previous measurement. (This will allow you to cut two panels, which will give you more use out of your fabric.)
8. Measure and cut your fabric into 1-foot-wide panels.
9. Draw freehand a scallop pattern down the entire length of the panel. Trim your pattern with pinking shears, creating a more festive edge.
10. Using clothespins, attach the panel to the PVC frame along the outside of the pipe and over the top of the curtain panels. (Don't worry about overlapping at the ends.)

Yes, you can: Since this project requires a large amount of fabric, we have chosen inexpensive ticking. Burlap or muslin would work well and is also inexpensive.

Rickracktoe

If you don't have time to read
your favorite youngsters a bedtime
story, you can lure them in between
the sheets with a quick game of
ticktacktoe. Use your bed cover
as a game board to attach your
movable X's and O's.

Supplies

Rickrack in multiple colors
Bias tape in multiple colors
Felt (enough to cut out all your X's
and O's)
2 paper plates
Duvet cover
Fabric glue

Tools

Scissors
Measuring tape
Rotary blade
Ruler

Getting Started

1. Spread out your duvet cover on
   a flat surface.
2. Design your ticktacktoe board
   by laying out the bias tape on
   the cover.
3. Cut the bias tape to the desired
   lengths. (We think it's fun for the
   vertical pieces to run the entire
   length of the duvet cover, and
   the horizontal pieces to run the
   entire width of the cover.)
4. Cut rickrack pieces the same
   length as your bias tape pieces.
5. Glue the bias tape onto the
   duvet cover, making sure the
   tape lies smooth.
6. Glue rickrack on top of bias tape.
7. Draw a template of your X's and
   O's on paper plates.
8. Cut out your templates.
9. Using your template, cut out felt
   X's and O's with your rotary
   blade, creating the pieces for
   your game board.

Happy Bed Skirt!

In order to keep goblins and monsters from crawling out from underneath the bed, we suggest you gussy up your child's bed skirt with pom-poms, buttons, and anything else that might convince your little one that no one except Harry Potter would pass underneath this protective shield.

Supplies
Fabric
Pom-poms
Buttons
Fabric glue

Tools
Glue gun and glue sticks
Iron and ironing board
Scissors
Tape measure

Getting Started
1. To make the three panels, measure the width and length of your bed.
2. Cut fabric in needed lengths adding an extra 3 inches to create a hem. Keep the natural width of the fabric.
3. Using fabric glue, make a hem 1½ inches long along the bottom edge and both ends of the panel.
4. Press your panels.
5. Attach pom-poms and buttons, in alternating sequence, with hot glue, approximately 4 inches above the hem, placing them every 8 inches or so on the fabric.
6. Slide the unhemmed edge of the panel underneath the mattress, leaving the decorated border hung evenly above the floor. You want to make sure your bed skirt barely touches the floor.
7. Continue for all three panels.

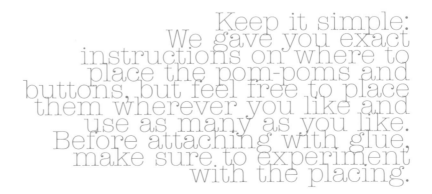

Keep it simple: We gave you exact instructions on where to place the pom-poms and buttons, but feel free to place them wherever you like and use as many as you like. Before attaching with glue, make sure to experiment with the placing.

Flying Trapeze

Remember the circus? My favorite act was the trapeze artists. If you have a youngster who also likes to fly, surprise him or her by making this trapeze bookcase for favorite toys to swing on.

Supplies

4 pieces of rope
5 precut wood shelves, 3 × 1 foot each
4 ceiling hooks

Tools

Drill
Pencil
Tape measure

Getting Started

1. Drill four holes in each shelf, two at each end. Each hole should be 4 inches in from end and 2 inches in from either side. Make sure the holes are big enough for the width of the rope.
2. Starting with the bottom shelf, push the rope through a hole.
3. Leave approximately 10 inches of rope below the shelf and tie it off in a knot.
4. Repeat steps 2 and 3 for the three remaining holes.
5. Make another knot in the rope 12 inches above the bottom shelf on all four pieces.
6. Feed the remaining rope through the next board.
7. Repeat steps 2–6 until final shelf is in place.
8. With a pencil, mark on the ceiling where the ceiling hooks go. They should form a rectangle, mimicking the placement of the shelves' holes so the rope will hang straight.
9. Secure hooks into ceiling.
10. Attach each rope to a hook with a knot.
11. Adjust knots accordingly on each shelf until level.

Here to stay: In 1859, the first flying trapeze act was performed by Jules Léotard, a French acrobat with the Cirque Napoléon. He didn't have a safety net. The body-hugging costume was later named after him.

Bed Knobs and Broomsticks

Anyone can put up a drapery rod, but how about letting your imagination go and thinking of what your child loves most? We took a hint from *Mary Poppins*, but you can also take clues from *Charlotte's Web* to create a weblike window covering or *Alice in Wonderland* for a looking-glass window.

Supplies

Push broom (1 for each window)
Assorted ribbon
Drapery rod holders (2 for each window, large enough to fit a broomstick handle)

Tools

Scissors
Tape measure

Getting Started

1. Attach drapery rod holders, using the instructions that came with the holders.
2. Choose your ribbons, alternating colors and patterns.
3. Measure the length of the window from top to bottom of the pane.
4. Measure and cut strips of ribbon to match window measurements. (Make sure to cut the ribbon 4 or 5 inches longer than needed. The extra length is what you will use to tie the ribbon to the broom handle.)
5. Create a loop at one end of the ribbon by tying it into a simple knot.
6. Slide your strips of ribbon onto the broom handle. (For an average-size window you want to use approximately twenty strips of ribbon; however, this number may vary, depending upon your taste.)
7. Place the broom with your ribbons attached into the drapery rod holders.
8. Trim the ends of the ribbon with pinking shears or on a slant for a more decorated look.

Pollock, Perhaps

Jackson Pollock knew how to make a statement, so for this project I borrowed his technique to give a bit of flair to an otherwise blank and boring window shade. Since Pollock followed no rules—some would say he just made a mess with the paint—this is a great project in which to get your little artist involved.

Supplies

Semigloss latex paint
Roll-up window shade (1 per window)

Tools

Paintbrush

Getting Started

1. On a flat surface, release the window shade until it is fully extended.
2. Dip your paintbrush into the paint. Don't completely immerse the brush; just dip it in enough to get some paint on the tip.
3. By flicking your wrist, splatter the paint across the shade.
4. Do this until you have achieved your desired pattern.
5. Dry thoroughly.
6. Follow hanging instructions and install.

Wet Paint!
Bright Lights!

One of my favorite places to stand is in front of a Sherman Williams color chip display. I stand there and imagine my rooms in all different colors. I confess—I also get excited about all the various painting supplies, brushes, drop cloths, and rollers, and the fact that stores give away free paper paint buckets really floats my boat. So start them young and show them the joys paint stores have to offer.

Supplies

Paper paint buckets
Electric cords with lightbulb fittings
(1 cord per bucket)
Lightbulbs
Hooks

Tools

Scissors

Getting Started

MAKING THE FIXTURE

1. Using the blade of the scissors, make a hole large enough to fit the plug end of the cord through the center of the bottom of your paint bucket.
2. Place bulb in the socket of the electric cord. (Use a low-wattage bulb to ensure safety.)
3. Feed and pull cord until the bulb is resting at the base of the bucket. (Fixture should hang from the cord.)
4. Repeat steps 1–3 for the number of lights you want to hang.

HANGING THE FIXTURE

5. There are many ways to hang this light: You can hang it from a hook on the wall or from a hook in the ceiling. We suggest you hang two or three in a group at varying heights.
6. Plug it in. It's that simple!

Yes, you can: Popcorn buckets would also add a nice touch.

Button Up

Lampshades are a great way to tie any room together, and we've echoed our ribbon and button theme in this shade design to underscore the overall look.

Supplies

Lampshade
Assorted buttons
1-inch grosgrain ribbon
½-inch grosgrain ribbon
Small pom-poms

Tools

Glue gun and glue sticks
Scissors

Getting Started

1. Cut the 1-inch ribbon into two pieces long enough to form an X on the shade.
2. Repeat step 1 until you have enough X's to go around your shade.
3. Glue the ribbon in place.
4. At the top and bottom of each ribbon, glue a button.
5. Create a rosette by winding the ½-inch ribbon back and forth in a figure-8 pattern.
6. Secure the ends with a dab of hot glue.
7. Glue a small pom-pom in the center of the rosette.
8. Glue the rosette onto a spot where the two 1-inch ribbons intersect.
9. Repeat steps 5–8 until all your X's have been decorated.

Sacks to Pack

I remember that when my little brother was young, he was always dragging around an old backpack. Kids love all kinds of bags and sacks to put their special treasures in. We've created one here that will do everything from storing toys to hiding dirty laundry. I guarantee grown-ups will like it too.

Supplies

1 piece of fabric, 60 × 56 inches
1 piece of ¾-inch rope, 6 feet long
Fabric glue

Tools

Tape measure

Get Started

1. On a flat surface, fold fabric in half. The side of the fabric you ultimately want showing should be inside the fold.
2. Using fabric glue, seal the two sides of your fabric, leaving 5 inches of fabric at the top unglued.
3. Create a sleeve for the rope by laying the rope along the top edge and folding over remaining fabric. Attach with fabric glue.
4. Let glue dry completely.
5. Turn fabric right side out and cinch rope into a loop. It's ready for hanging.

Keep it simple: Choose washable fabric so that your pup's perch will always be fresh.

Dog's Best Friend

You've had some fun getting the room ready for your favorite child, but what about your child's favorite canine?

Supplies

Fabric or fabric remnants
Foam batting
Adhesive Velcro
Fabric glue

Tools

Scissors

Getting Started

1. To create a quiltlike effect, put the first piece of fabric pattern side down, and put your second piece pattern side down, slightly overlapping the first. Create a square with the pieces.
2. Make a line of fabric glue down one edge and press the other edge on top. Hold together until secure.

3. Repeat steps 1 and 2 until the top and bottom pieces are complete.
4. Take your top and bottom piece and again place them on top of each other, pattern side down.
5. Using fabric glue, connect three sides together.
6. On the fourth side place strips of Velcro in order to seal this end.
7. Stuff your pet's bed with batting.

LIVING ROOM

Sole Mate

In this project I wanted to re-create
the floor of my childhood playroom—
a fantastic black-and-white tile.
We found a great material at our
local shoe repair shop, a durable
and easy-to-clean rubber shoe sole
fiber. It has a great nonslip surface
for those games of musical chairs
that get out of hand. We suspect this
would even stop that spilled glass
of milk from breaking when it hits
the floor. Need I say more?

Supplies

Sheets of black rubber shoe sole
material (we used 4- × 18-inch
rectangular sheets)
Precut self-adhesive white linoleum
squares
Rubber glue

Getting Started

1. Remove all furniture from room.
   Make sure the floor is clean
   and dry.
2. Lay out the black rubber mats
   and white linoleum squares in
   the desired pattern.
3. Starting from a corner of the
   room, glue the squares to the
   floor. Press down to ensure
   proper setting.

Make it chic:
Shoe material comes in
many patterns. Mix and
match them to create
another fun aspect of
your floor covering.

Rule of thumb: Another term for wainscoting is "dado," which describes the lower portion of the wall of a room decorated differently from the upper section.

Stripe Up the Band

Want to keep the kids from drawing on your walls? Give them their own wall. We divided ours in half by painting the top portion in bright stripes and the bottom with that great chalkboard paint that you can find at almost any home improvement store. Just keep in mind how tall your children are, since you want the chalkboard portion to be at the right height for their doodles.

Supplies

Chalkboard paint
2 colors of semigloss latex paint
White semigloss latex paint
Molding
Baseboard
Finishing nails

Tools

Paint roller
Paint tray
Painter's tape
Hammer
Pencil
Tape measure

Getting Started

1. Make sure walls are clean.
2. Measuring from the floor up, mark with a pencil the desired height of the chalkboard section of your wall. (Remember, this is the time to take into consideration the size of the little person or people.)
3. Tape the perimeter of the room at this desired height.
4. Apply the chalkboard paint below the taped-off area. Let dry.
5. Divide the top half of the room into horizontal stripes and mark them with a pencil. (Our stripes are approximately 1 foot wide, but the math will vary, depending on the dimensions of your room.)
6. Choose which stripes will be in which color.
7. For the first set of stripes that will be painted all the same color, apply painter's tape to the top and the bottom, outlining the area that will be painted.
8. Apply the paint in between the taped-off area.
9. Let dry and remove tape.
10. Repeat steps 7–9 for the second set of stripes, which will be painted in a different color.
11. Paint the molding and baseboard with white paint. Let dry.
12. Using hammer and nails, attach molding to the wall, dividing the striped half from the chalkboard half.
13. Using hammer and nails, attach baseboard to the wall.

Clearly Covered

Sticky fingers, greasy hands. . . . We came up with a great way to protect the furniture and add a splash of color to your most basic sofa.

Supplies

Clear plastic vinyl
Sturdy cotton fabric

Tools

Staple gun and staples
Tape measure
Scissors

Get Started

1. Measure the width of the sofa.
2. Divide this measurement in half. You will need to create two separate pieces, one for the left side of the sofa and the other for the right.
3. Measure and cut the two pieces of fabric approximately 8 inches less than the width of the previous measurements, but long enough so that the fabric can wrap all the way around the back of the sofa and down to the front. Do the same with the plastic.
4. Remove the seat cushions from the sofa.
5. Starting at the front of the sofa, staple the plastic and the fabric into place underneath the sofa.
6. Replace the seat cushions to hold fabric with plastic in place.
7. Pull the fabric with plastic over the back cushion continuing over the back of the sofa, and secure it in place underneath with a staple gun.
8. You can repeat these steps to cover the arms of the sofa or matching armchair and throw pillows. (We did both.)

Rule of thumb: The plastic used in this project is the same material used in plastic tablecloths. It can be cleaned with a damp rag or window cleaner.

Getting Started

1. Starting with your tabletop, measure length and width, remembering to add enough length to fold under the lip of the tabletop.

2. Cut the contact paper using your measurements and apply to top of the table.

3. Measure and cut enough contact paper to cover all four sides of the table, including a little extra to fold under, and apply to the table.

4. With a piece of paper, measure and cut a template for the legs of the table. (If your table has square legs your template will have four pieces. If the legs are round, your template will be one piece.)

5. Using your template, cut out the contact paper pieces to fit on the legs and apply.

On Contact!

Take that old flea market find or basic blah coffee table and make it fun with some really cool contact paper. It's inexpensive and easy to re-cover when your youngster tires of one pattern and is ready for the next.

Supplies
Contact paper
Plain coffee table
Paper

Tools
Scissors
Utility knife
Ruler
Tape measure

Make it chic: Depending on the pattern you choose, try to match up the pattern as you go.

Drapery Dress

Turn that frown upside down.
How? By turning those plain drapes
into something to smile about,
with striped ticking and some
bright-colored yarn.

Supplies

Premade tab curtains and valances
(1 for each window)
Yarn
Fabric in a ticking stripe
Fabric glue

Tools

Pinking shears
Tape measure
Steam iron and ironing board

Getting Started

1. Measure desired width and
   length of the trim you would
   like to add to your curtains
   and valance. The trim's width
   should be the same, and the
   length is up to your discretion.
   (Think of it as a band around
   the bottom that works as an
   accent or adds length.)
2. Using pinking shears, cut
   ticking stripe fabric to your
   specification.
3. Press curtains and valance.
4. Apply the fabric glue along the
   top edge of the ticking stripe
   fabric and attach to the bottom
   half of the valance.

5. Attach small pieces of yarn in
   the shape of a bow or knot
   every 6 inches along the top of
   your ticking stripe trim. (You will
   need about six bows or knots for
   each valance.)
6. Repeat step 5, creating another
   row of bows along the bottom
   half of the ticking stripe trim.

Yes, you can:
Trim your
curtains
with fabric
from old
tablecloths
or linens. It's
a great way
to give old
treasures a
new life and
a great way
to add length
to curtains
that are too
short.

Mop Top

Now that we've made the curtains,
let's find something fun to hang
them on. And you thought that
mop was just for cleaning up
spilled juice . . .

Supplies

Rag mop heads (1 for each
window)
Mop handle (1 for each mop)
Drapery rod holders (2 for each
window, wide enough to hold mop
handle)

Tools

Screwdriver

Getting Started

1. Attach drapery rod holders
   to either side of the window,
   using the directions that came
   with them.
2. Slide your curtains onto the
   mop handles.
3. Attach mop head.
4. Place the mop with head
   attached in the drapery rod
   holders, with the mop head
   falling to the outside of
   the window.

Battery-Operated

When I was a little girl, my mom would take down the chandelier in the dining room to clean it every spring, and I would just marvel at all the crystals and how they sparkled. Well, with a few tools from your local hardware store you too can create a special chandelier for your youngster, made with one thing that I know kids love: flashlights.

Supplies

5 matching flashlights with batteries
2 stainless steel vegetable steamers, in different sizes
Heavy-gauge wire
5 hose clamps (wide enough to fit around flashlights)
Ceiling hook
Vise grips

Tools

Wire cutters
Screwdriver
Tape measure

Getting Started

1. Put batteries in flashlights.
2. Attach the hose clamps to the handle of the flashlights, making sure they are tight.
3. Take your larger vegetable steamer and, using the vise grips, attach flashlights evenly spaced around the outside of the steamer. (Our larger steamer was approximately 8 inches in diameter, so we used five flashlights.)
4. Measure the space between the larger steamer and where the smaller one will hang. (We left a space of 10 inches between the steamers.)

5. Using your previous measurements, cut the wire and connect the smaller steamer by looping a piece of the wire through the steamer's perforated bottom. Pull the wire down and attach it to the top of one of the vise grips that are connected to the edge of the larger steamer (twisting the wire tightly to secure).
6. Repeat step 5 until wire is connected to all five vise grips.
7. Adjust wire as needed until your light fixture feels balanced.
8. Place a ceiling hook in the ceiling.
9. Measure the desired length from the hook to where you want the chandelier to hang.
10. Using your measurements, cut two pieces of wire.
11. Attach the two pieces of wire on opposite sides of the steamer by twisting the wire securely through the perforated bottom.
12. Hang the chandelier on the hook by twisting the two wire ends around it.

Make it chic: Alternate flashlights in bold colors. For a modern look, use all stainless steel flashlights.

Pillow Talk

Remember that great sofa covering
we dreamed up earlier in this
section? Well, you can do the same
thing for your throw pillows. Sticky
fingers and greasy hands beware.

Supplies
Clear, heavy-duty plastic
Fabric
Pillow forms
Large safety pins (3 or 4 per pillow)

Tools
Scissors
Tape measure

Getting Started
1. Measure the length and width
   of the pillow forms.
2. Using these measurements,
   cut one piece of fabric large
   enough to cover both sides of
   the pillow form.
3. Wrap pillow form in fabric just
   as you would wrap a present.
4. Use safety pins to hold fabric
   in place.
5. Cut plastic in strips, long
   enough to wrap around the
   entire pillow and approximately
   3 inches shorter in width than
   the width of the pillow.
6. Pin the plastic together in the
   back with safety pins.

Here to stay: Change the
art in your frames every
season, or even every
month. Keep aspiring
artists in your house well
represented in your
family's personal gallery.

Kids' Gallery

My parents always made me
feel special whenever they hung
my artwork alongside some of
their favorite paintings. Give your
little ones that same sensation.
When you run out of room on the
refrigerator, create a gallery of
your children's work. And when
you're done hanging all their
wares, invite their friends over
for a real gallery opening.

Supplies
Black 11- × 14-inch document
frames (number varies according
to room size)
Kids' artwork (large enough to fill
the frames)
Nails

Tools
Utility knife
Hammer
Tape measure

Getting Started
1. Remove glass from frame.
2. Place glass on top of artwork.
3. Using your utility knife, trim
   artwork to fit frame.
   (You'll want to do this on a
   scratchproof surface.)
4. Reinsert art, glass, and back
   matter into frame.
5. Hang frames side by side to
   create a symmetrical look.

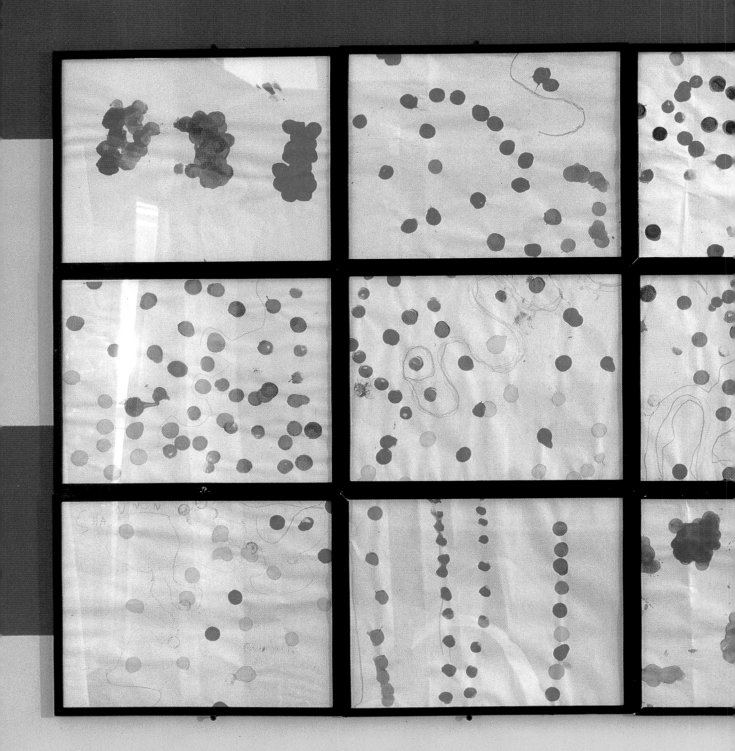

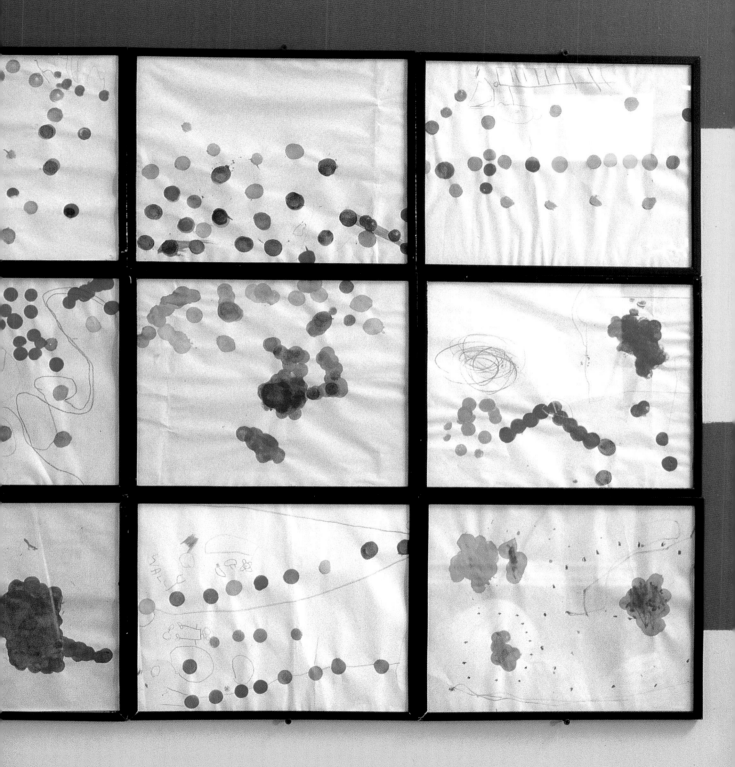

RESOURCES

How to find the materials used throughout *KATIE BROWN decorates*

HARDWARE, LUMBER, AND PAINT

Lowe's Home Improvement Warehouse

For store locations, call 800-44-LOWES or visit www.lowes.com.

FURNITURE

IKEA

For store locations, call 800-434-4532 or visit www.ikea.com.

FABRIC

Sanderson

For availability, call 212-319-7220.

HOME ACCESSORIES

Lenox Inc.

For store locations, call 800-63-LENOX or visit www.lenox.com.

CRAFT SUPPLIES

Jo-Ann etc.

For store locations, call 888-739-4120 or visit www.joann.com.

Thanks to Jo-Ann etc. for providing materials used in the home decorating projects in this book.
Jo-Ann etc. is owned by Jo-Ann Stores, Inc., which owns and operates close to 1,000 stores nationwide under
the names Jo-Ann etc. and Jo-Ann Fabrics and Crafts.